I0031843

ON TAUNGURUNG LAND

SHARING HISTORY AND CULTURE

Aboriginal History Incorporated

Aboriginal History Inc. is a part of the Australian Centre for Indigenous History, Research School of Social Sciences, The Australian National University, and gratefully acknowledges the support of the School of History and the National Centre for Indigenous Studies, The Australian National University. Aboriginal History Inc. is administered by an Editorial Board which is responsible for all unsigned material. Views and opinions expressed by the author are not necessarily shared by Board members.

Contacting Aboriginal History

All correspondence should be addressed to the Editors, Aboriginal History Inc., ACIH, School of History, RSSS, 9 Fellows Road (Coombs Building), The Australian National University, Acton, ACT, 2601, or aboriginalhistoryinc@gmail.com.

WARNING: Readers are notified that this publication may contain names or images of deceased persons.

ON TAUNGURUNG LAND

SHARING HISTORY AND CULTURE

**UNCLE ROY PATTERSON
AND JENNIFER JONES**

Australian
National
University

PRESS

ANU PRESS

Published by ANU Press and Aboriginal History Inc.
The Australian National University
Acton ACT 2601, Australia
Email: anupress@anu.edu.au

Available to download for free at press.anu.edu.au

ISBN (print): 9781760464066
ISBN (online): 9781760464073

WorldCat (print): 1224453432
WorldCat (online): 1224452874

DOI: 10.22459/OTL.2020

This title is published under a Creative Commons Attribution-NonCommercial-NoDerivatives 4.0 International (CC BY-NC-ND 4.0).

The full licence terms are available at
creativecommons.org/licenses/by-nc-nd/4.0/legalcode

Cover design and layout by ANU Press

Cover photograph: Patterson family photograph, circa 1904

This edition © 2020 ANU Press and Aboriginal History Inc.

Contents

Acknowledgements

The research and publication of this book was made possible by the following grants and generous collaborations:

- La Trobe University Publication Award Scheme, which funded Moorina Bonini's photography. Thank you Moorina for your wonderful images and company during our bush lessons with Uncle Roy.
- The Public Record Office Victoria – Local History Grants Program, GA-F20909-9017. This successful grant application was made possible by the generosity of my collaborators at Murrindindi Shire Council, who administered the grant. Sincere thanks to Libby Kotschet, Murrindindi Library Service and the Alexandra Friends of the Library for their assistance, support and encouragement.
- The staff at Camp Jungai provided access to their beautiful Rubicon Valley site and willing support, as it was required.
- My thanks to the anonymous referees whose clear and constructive suggestions drove improvements to the manuscript.
- Thanks to Chris Marshall from Taungurung Land & Waters Council who generously read and checked the manuscript for errors. Thanks also to Joanne Honeysett for her timely and sensitive cultural advice.
- Rani Kerin, Monographs Editor, Aboriginal History Inc., offered ready advice and expert copyediting. Thank you Rani.
- Thanks to Rebecca Le Get for sharing your skills and expertise by preparing the map.
- Special thanks to Sam and Keith Patterson for providing hospitality, family photographs, advice and assistance after Uncle Roy's death.

This book is dedicated to Taungurung Elders, past, present and emerging.

Note on terminology

There are many variations of spelling for the Aboriginal nation Taungurung. For consistency and to minimise confusion, in this book I adopt the spelling used by the Taungurung Land and Waters Council (Aboriginal Corporation), the Registered Aboriginal Party. Common variations include Taunerong, Daunarung and Daun Wurrung. Uncle Roy preferred 'Daunarung', so I use this spelling in his direct speech.

Preface

The unprecedented and devastating bushfires experienced across vast areas of eastern Australia in the long summer of 2019–20 drew world attention to the fragility of Australia's ancient ecosystems. Many now acknowledge that climate change, drought and the cumulative effect of inappropriate settler land management practices have made Australia's bush and grasslands increasingly vulnerable to wildfires. In the aftermath of the disaster, some commentators called for the revival of Indigenous cultural burning to reduce the risk of wildfire in south-eastern Australia. In the past decade, collaboration between environmental agencies, government and Traditional Owners has seen the restoration of cultural burning practices in northern Australia.[1] Such cultural resurgence holds potential benefits for people and places across the whole continent of Australia, not just in the north. Traditional Owners hold sophisticated ecological knowledge that explains the interrelationships between 'people, plants, animals, landforms and celestial bodies'.[2] This place-based wisdom is both practical and spiritual, and directs proper action or 'right behaviour' on that particular land.[3] Colonial records reveal the fury and distress of Traditional Owners when settlers contravened traditional laws by using agricultural and forestry methods most appropriate to Europe.[4] This included using fire incorrectly for Australian conditions or failing to understand the importance of timely or controlled burning.[5] Yet, because settlers commonly believed First Nations people were 'primitive' and ignorant, they did not recognise or respect their place-based Indigenous knowledge. A memoir by Marion Popple (1872–1960), a settler woman who lived near Taggerty in the Upper Goulburn Valley of central Victoria,

---

1   McKemey et al., 'Cross-Cultural Monitoring'.
2   Grieves, 'Aboriginal Spirituality', 365.
3   Broome, 'There Were Vegetables'.
4   Kenny, 'Broken Treaty'.
5   Fred Cahir et al., 'Winda Lingo Parugoneit'.

provides an example. Popple wrote her memoir in 1936, recalling childhood memories and stories told by early settlers. 'The blackfellows', she wrote:

> Always called the [Mount] Cathedral 'Debils Jawbone'. They were afraid whenever they heard the wind roaring through the caves and gullies, and they used to tell us that 'one day big fellow fire him all burn up'[;] they would roll their eyes and show the whites, poor blacks really believed it would happen.[6]

Dire warnings that deadly wildfire would transform the Cathedral Range were trivialised by Europeans, whose cultural superiority led them to dismiss the ancient wisdom of the Traditional Owners, the Taungurung people. These predictions came to fruition when wildfire swept through the district during the Black Friday disaster of 1939, and during the Black Saturday fires of 2009, when the bulk of the Cathedral Range State Park was burnt. These unnamed Taungurung people from 'the early days', I suggest, were not afraid of the 'wind roaring through the caves and gullies', as Marion Popple implied. Rather, they feared the outcomes of exploitative and extractive land management strategies that seemed to disregard the needs of plants and animals, land and waters.

Uncle Roy Patterson was a Taungurung Elder who inherited detailed traditional ecological knowledge from his ancestors. He believed that settler practices were harming the land and shared the worldwide concern of Indigenous people that injustices arise 'when one culture decides what is significant and worth protecting in the heritage of another'.[7] Uncle Roy's priority was, therefore, to educate as many people as possible about his beautiful country. Before he died on 15 April 2017, he shared his generational knowledge of bush tucker and bush medicine with anyone who would listen: school children, community groups and academics like me. During one of our trips looking for bush tucker, Uncle Roy took me to Mount Monda, 920 metres above sea level in the Yarra Ranges National Park. It was a cool December morning and the mountainside rang with bird calls. Uncle Roy quipped:

---

6   'Some True Stories about the Aborigines of Victoria for Vivienne Hulley and Audrey Bevan, Read by Mrs Marion Popple of Wymarong', Aborigines of Australia—Miscellaneous Reminiscences, Royal Historical Society of Victoria, MS 22545, Box 118/11.
7   Susemihl, 'We Are Key Players'.

Isn't it gorgeous up here; that is Wurundjeri land up there and this is Daunarung over here. You can drive all the way along here and all you got is mountain pepper [trees]. Because the eucalyptus and mountain ash gets clear felled, all this will go, and we will lose the mountain pepper as well. So, it is not just the animals and the reptiles and that, it is the trees with our bush tucker and bush medicine as well that we lose. There is the ring tail possum, the bushy tail possum, the yellow tail black cockatoo, the red tail black cockatoo and the little glider. There is the rock wallaby and a little black swamp wallaby; the porcupine, the wombat; all native animals that live in this area and are going to die and near be extinct if we don't stop it. Australia is Aboriginal Country, not the Europeans' country; they reckon that they own it, but they don't ... It is terrifying what Europeans want to do to our beautiful Country ... I better not go any further or I'll get real savage about it![8]

This book reveals why Uncle Roy's ecological convictions were so strong. We first chart his family story, and the wider experience of the Taungurung Nation under colonial rule, and then share the distinctive and vibrant living knowledge that has been handed down to Uncle Roy from generation to generation. Uncle Roy's final wish was to facilitate healing and growth for all Australians by sharing this heritage. Therefore, our book attempts to reduce environmental harms and foster ecological justice by teaching wider audiences about Taungurung land and revitalising relationships with local places.

Jennifer Jones
May 2020

---

8   Roy Patterson, in conversation with Jennifer Jones, 14 December 2016, DS300172–74. All transcripts are in the author's possession.

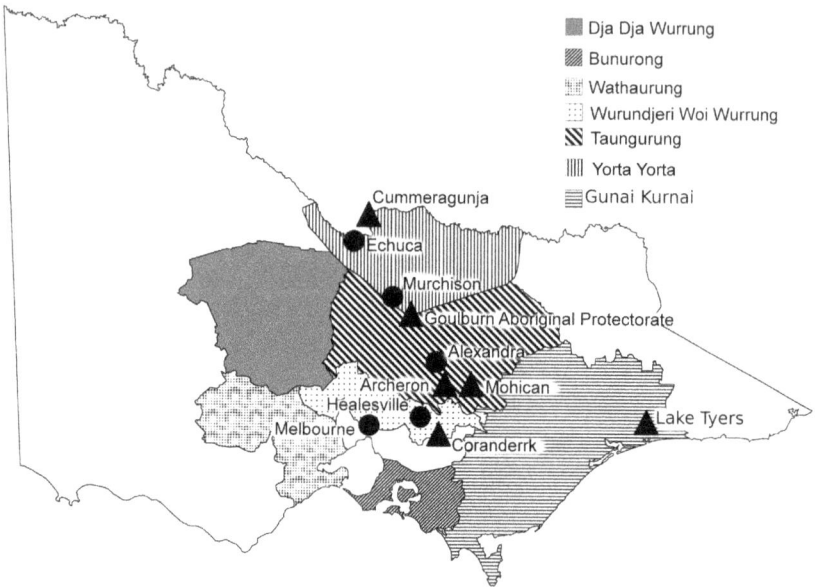

Dja Dja Wurrung
Bunurong
Wathaurung
Wurundjeri Woi Wurrung
Taungurung
Yorta Yorta
Gunai Kurnai

Cummeragunja
Echuca
Murchison
Goulburn Aboriginal Protectorate
Alexandra
Archeron
Mohican
Healesville
Lake Tyers
Melbourne
Coranderrk

Map identifying First Nations peoples and location of Acheron, Mohican, Coranderrk, Cummeragunja and Lake Tyers Aboriginal stations

Triangles = Aboriginal protectorate and Aboriginal Stations; Circles = Towns and cities; Patterned squares = Lands of the Kulin Nation and that of adjacent Nations discussed in this book.

Source: Rebecca Le Get.

Introduction: Meeting and working with Uncle Roy

In mid-2015 a friend of Uncle Roy's, who was an acquaintance of a colleague of mine, approached me to co-author this book. At the time I was on study leave and visiting the National Library of Scotland. I was reading letters written by a Scottish widow left destitute and far from home when her husband died of mining-related chest disease on the central Victorian goldfields in 1869. I was fully immersed in that project, and the widow's plight seemed a world away from Taggerty and this stranger named Roy Patterson. I was to discover, however, that the crimson cords of Empire did connect these apparently disparate people, as they also linked Uncle Roy to me.

This Scottish family had made their home at Bendigo during the gold rush and were living on the traditional lands of Uncle Roy's great-grandmother, Dja Dja Wurrung woman Emma Kerr. Emma was about 16 years old when she gave birth to Uncle Roy's grandfather, John Patterson, to the north of Bendigo, also in 1869. Emma Kerr's childhood had been shaped by the dramatic population boom fostered by gold. The end of the rush would similarly dictate her adult choices. As the masses of enriched and disappointed diggers sought new occupations, the colony of Victoria was under pressure to open pastoral land for closer settlement. Vast squatting runs were carved into smaller farmsteads and these settlers called for the segregation and control of Aboriginal people. Voluntary Aboriginal protectorates and missions had already failed to satisfy such demands. So, in 1869, the colony of Victoria became the first Australian government to design coercive legislation for the management of Aboriginal people. Passed on 11 November 1869, it shaped the lives of Emma Kerr's newborn son, her grandchildren and great-grandchildren. The *Aboriginal Protection Act 1869 (Vic)*, also known as an *Act for the Protection and Management of the Aboriginal Natives of Victoria*, delivered powers to regulate every aspect of the lives of Aboriginal people in the colony.[1] In subsequent years, this Act was amended to enable extraordinary levels of control over Emma Kerr's place of residence, her employment and income, her marriage and her social life. This legislation would eventually force her children into a dormitory at Coranderrk Aboriginal Station and curtail their education. The amendments of 1886, colloquially known as the 'Half-Caste Act', split Aboriginal families apart. Those with mixed racial heritage were forced to merge into mainstream society and local reserves were closed, concentrating Aboriginal residents on the remaining faraway Aboriginal stations. These government measures made it difficult for Aboriginal Elders to pass on traditional knowledge. Uncle Roy Patterson's retention of Taungurung cultural knowledge is, therefore, a notable achievement, given this challenging experience of nearly 150 years duration.

Meeting Uncle Roy

When I drove down the Maroondah Highway to meet Uncle Roy at Taggerty for the first time, I intended to decline his request to help write this book. I was focused on the goldfields project and thought I was already overcommitted. Somehow, to my surprise, it only took Uncle Roy 10 minutes to change my thinking. Uncle Roy described his ambition for this book and made a simple pitch:

> I've had a full life, a good life, but now I want to get the knowledge that my grandmother and grandfather taught me, and what I've learnt over the years from Aboriginal people, to other people so that they can learn it, including Daunarung people and my family all around here. This is the reason I want to write this book, to get that knowledge out there. They have got to learn it and get some of their history and culture back. Without culture, you've got nothing. This is why I want to write this book. Any information you want, I'll give it gladly, if you write it for me.[2]

---

1   *Aboriginal Protection Act 1869 (Vic)*, accessed 7 February 2019, www.foundingdocs.gov.au/item-sdid-22.html.

2   Spelt Taungurung by the Taungurung Land and Waters Council (Aboriginal Corporation), the Registered Aboriginal Party, but also spelt Taunerong, Daunarung and Daun Wurrung. Uncle Roy preferred 'Daunarung', so I use this spelling in his direct speech. Roy Patterson, in conversation with Jennifer Jones, 3 March 2016, DS3001137.

Then 75 years old, Uncle Roy wanted to secure his cultural knowledge for future generations. He had already outlived most Aboriginal men by nearly a decade.[3] I felt my resolve weaken, and my cup of tea wasn't even tepid by the time I'd agreed to his proposal.

Working with Uncle Roy

We agreed that I would come back to Taggerty at regular intervals to help us get to know each other and to record Taungurung generational knowledge. Whenever my work required travel from Wodonga to Melbourne, I detoured via Healesville on the way home. I would stay overnight and spend the next day with Uncle Roy in the Upper Goulburn Valley. We usually met at the Taggerty shop, sharing toasted sandwiches and a cup of tea before I turned on the digital recorder. We would chat about Taungurung culture, Patterson family history, and Uncle Roy's knowledge of bush tucker and bush medicine. After a decade working as a cultural educator with school students, TAFE students and with community groups, Uncle Roy hoped to reach wider audiences with this book. His vision was that traditional ecological knowledge would cultivate respect for Taungurung culture and foster new habits of care for Country. He was ambitious, he wanted to shape Australia's future:

> I want this book to get out to people that I don't teach and schools I don't get near, to museums and universities that know nothing about it. It will be something to show about our culture.[4]

Uncle Roy believed that encounters with significant Aboriginal places and place-based knowledge could be transformative for both Aboriginal and non-Aboriginal people. Recalling numerous trips leading school children to a special site, he noted:

> When I take you up there you will experience it too. It is an enormous, beautiful feeling. To tell the honest truth, you won't want to leave there because of the feeling you get, and I love it, it is so bloody beautiful. Every time I take a school up there, I take

---

3   Life expectancy at birth for Aboriginal and Torres Strait Islander males is estimated to be 67.2 years, 11.5 years less than life expectancy at birth for non-Indigenous males (78.7 years). 'The Health and Welfare of Australia's Aboriginal and Torres Strait Islander Peoples', accessed 7 February 2019, www.abs.gov.au/AUSSTATS/abs@.nsf/lookup/4704.0Chapter218Oct+2010.
4   Roy Patterson, in conversation with Jennifer Jones, Taggerty, 3 March 2016, DS3001139.

the students to show them and let them experience it. They love it. It might be a little different for non-Aboriginal people, but those kids tell me what they feel, and they love it.[5]

Uncle Roy believed that everyone could appreciate the spiritual significance of Aboriginal land. While this education would obviously be different for non-Aboriginal people, Uncle Roy wanted everyone to 'learn what I have learnt and how I have learnt it. I am teaching our Old People's way, not the European way'. This included me. After several meetings talking about his family history and heritage, he said:

> We've talked about bush tucker and bush medicine, now we've got to get out onto the land and do it! We've got to get out onto the land where the plants are, to get the feel of it and the knowledge of it. Talking is alright, practise is better! Everything you see, it all belongs to the Aboriginal culture and the Dreamtime.[6]

We took to the road, looking for seasonal bush tucker and bush medicine plants. Every time we met, Uncle Roy would test my comprehension and assimilation of previous lessons. 'So', he would say, 'what else do you want to know?'

Some months into my Taungurung education another pattern emerged in our collaboration. I began to visit archives in Melbourne to read the European historic record, and afterwards I would meet Uncle Roy to discuss the historic characters and incidents I had encountered. Uncle Roy would then test the veracity of these European perspectives against his generational oral knowledge. While agreeing that historic records could be useful, he believed that they had to be adequately contextualised by Taungurung perspectives and the known experience of his ancestors. He explained:

> We never wrote nothing down, so I don't know if it is true or not; if I can't get any feeling for it, I don't know whether it is just made up. If it was the truth, I'd get a feeling for it.[7]

---

5   Roy Patterson, in conversation with Jennifer Jones, 3 March 2016, DS3001139.
6   Roy Patterson, in conversation with Jennifer Jones, 15 April 2016, DS300143.
7   Roy Patterson, in conversation with Jennifer Jones, 15 April 2016, DS300143.

This 'feeling' for historic truth relied upon spiritual communication with the Old People and the consensus foundation of Aboriginal oral history. Uncle Roy's extension of trust in my skills and experience as a historian also played a role. I returned transcripts for Uncle Roy to check and we clarified details, but otherwise Uncle Roy left the writing and collation of the book to me. He was firm, however, in his decision that the book was not a biography. Uncle Roy was a recovered alcoholic, and he was not proud of all the choices he had made in his lifetime. He was conscious that some of his past actions had hurt other people and that these stories were not his to tell. Uncle Roy wanted to leave a positive legacy, centring on inherited cultural knowledge and the proud history of his ancestors. Therefore, the sections of this book that chart his personal history relate directly to his acquisition of bush skills or his carriage of traditional knowledge. He couldn't fix past mistakes, but he was taking future-oriented action within his realm of influence. He wanted to foster cultural revitalisation, by teaching:

> A way of life that children can grow up with and they do it later on in their lives and teach their children what they learnt, the way they learnt. There is no argument, no fight; it's beautiful harmony. I want to get it started again, to let the Aboriginal people know that this is our life without alcohol and drugs. If I can do that little bit, I've done something in my life.[8]

Although I did not recognise it at the time, I can see now that Uncle Roy was preparing for his death. The completion of our oral history yarns and seasonal journeys to see bush tucker came as a huge relief to him. He reflected on our collaboration:

> After the first meeting we had, I felt the eagerness come back in here, back into me heart. This is why I am so keen to show you anything you want to learn about and talk about. I am very proud and honoured to be doing it.[9]

Uncle Roy was widely respected for the depth of his cultural knowledge and he carried this inheritance with authority. He was not afraid to 'have a bit of a barney' with individuals or institutions who had incorrect information or who had failed, in his estimation, to observe the right

---

8   Roy Patterson, in conversation with Jennifer Jones, 3 March 2016, DS3001138.
9   Roy Patterson, in conversation with Jennifer Jones, 29 April 2016, DS300145–47.

protocols. He was protective of his cultural heritage and could be belligerent in defence of Taungurung rights. In areas outside his domain of authority, however, Uncle Roy preferred not to venture an opinion. If he was uncertain, he would shrug his shoulders and remain silent. That said, he was generally sceptical about the 'the university mob', particularly archaeologists who he believed had exploited Aboriginal cultural heritage. In such cases, he said: 'university rules go against my grain'. Uncle Roy was suspicious of European systems of government and knowledge production, but he was prepared to extend trust where he observed respect for Aboriginal traditional knowledge, adherence to cultural protocols and willingness to learn. Uncle Roy positioned himself as a lifelong learner:

> I've got a lot more to learn me self. It is a lifetime of learning; you never stop learning in Aboriginal life. I don't know about you Europeans, but we Aboriginal people, we learn all the time.[10]

But he also wryly observed: 'If you don't want to give respect out, you are not likely to get it back. That's the way of life my grandmother told me about, back in the early 1940s.'[11] Uncle Roy was therefore critical of the motives of non-Aboriginal people who sought Indigenous knowledge for personal gain, and he was selective about the extent of knowledge he shared. He told a story about 'a bloke he took up the mountain' on a bush tucker walk 'who was amazed' by what he saw:

> He said, 'I didn't know there was so much stuff up 'ere!' and I said, 'it is all bush tucker and bush medicine, old fella!' He is a man who has got a nursery in the Yarra Valley, and he tried to pick my brain, but I won't let him do it. He wants all the knowledge about native plants, but we get nothing out of it. We don't want royalties, we want acknowledgement. Royalties is nothing, acknowledgement of [traditional] knowledge is what I am talkin' about. That is the way I work: do you blame me? I want the knowledge out there in black and white so everybody can read it.[12]

Uncle Roy died before we had decided on a final structure for this book. In subsequent years I have made choices about the shape of the manuscript, first by reflecting on Uncle Roy's intentions and by consulting his family and members of the Taungurung community. Uncle Roy's overarching

10   Roy Patterson, in conversation with Jennifer Jones, 15 April 2016, DS300143.
11   Roy Patterson, in conversation with Jennifer Jones, 15 April 2016, DS300143.
12   Roy Patterson, in conversation with Jennifer Jones, 15 April 2016, DS300143.

desire was to see Taungurung knowledge and experience recognised and preserved. I have, therefore, chosen to present this work in two sections to highlight our distinct cultures and voices. The first section of the book, Chapters 1–5, draws mainly on archival research and is written in my scholarly voice. Here I provide a detailed account of Taungurung history since invasion. My focus is on settler policies of 'protection' as they affected Taungurung people and Uncle Roy's ancestors. I also highlight the decisions of relevant white settlers and officials. My aim is to contextualise the knowledge that Uncle Roy shares by developing a biographical and historical picture of the settlers with whom Taungurung people interacted. Understanding how officials and settlers interpreted and applied government policy assists a full appreciation of Aboriginal survival and adaptation, particularly how Taungurung customs and knowledge were maintained in post-contact society. The second section of the book, Chapters 6–8, focuses on Taungurung cultural knowledge as passed down to Uncle Roy. These chapters are primarily written in Uncle Roy's voice, and relate his generational knowledge of bush tucker, bush medicine and Taungurung cultural practices.

When Uncle Roy died, people asked me if I could finish the book without him. Perhaps the answer should have been 'no'. Yet, it was clear when we started the project that Uncle Roy envisaged future audiences reading his book. I decided to persist. I hope that he would have been proud of the final product.

PART 1: SHARING TAUNGURUNG HISTORY

1

An overview of Taungurung history since invasion

Uncle Roy was well known as a 'character' and he liked to have a laugh. He poked fun at white Australian society, criticised politicians, celebrated Aboriginal culture and instigated pride. He made a cheeky joke of serious topics such as the European classification of Aboriginal people according to caste. Aboriginal marriage and lineage traditions were designed to support the viability of the family and clan. In Uncle Roy's words, choice of marriage partner aimed to keep 'genetics fresh in the tribe'.[1] Under the pressure of European settlement, however, these core relationships became the basis for discrimination. Uncle Roy recalls his own embeddedness in family, and how this was interpreted by outsiders:

> Me grandfather was John William Banjo Patterson, he come from up north from near Deniliquin. Me grandmother was Elizabeth (Lizzie) Edmonds Patterson. She was a beautiful lady; I carry her in here [indicates heart]. Later I'll tell you how she made me an Elder at nine and a half years old. She was a Daunarung woman from up near Wangaratta. She married my grandfather up in Cummeragunja up in New South Wales, he was Wiradjuri and Dja Dja Wurrung. Wiradjuri land goes all the way up to Dubbo. His mother was Emma Kerr, she was Dja Dja Wurrung; she come from Bendigo Creek. In them days you went through your mother's

1   Roy Patterson, in conversation with Jennifer Jones, 12 July 2016, DS300157.

tribal area, not your father's. John William and Lizzie had seven children, including Frank, my father who married Violet Stephens, she was Irish. That makes me 'half-caste'.[2]

Uncle Roy gave a nudge and a wink as he made this last statement, about being 'half-caste'. So, I asked him to explain 'which half is which?' Laughing, he said, 'I go this way!' indicating an invisible line from head to toe. 'I've got this half Irish', he says, indicating his left side, 'and this half Aboriginal!', indicating his right.

Uncle Roy mobilised racist terminology to critique the fractionalisation of Aboriginality according to admixture of 'blood'.[3] People designated 'half-caste', like Uncle Roy and his family, were not officially categorised as Aboriginal by government, but the white community discriminated against them anyway. Uncle Roy's joke shows why Aboriginality is best defined according to cultural identification and community recognition.[4]

Uncle Roy Patterson identified as a Taungurung man, but he also acknowledged Dja Dja Wurrung, Wiradjuri and Irish heritage. The Taungurung clans belong to the Kulin Nation. Clans in this confederacy spoke related languages, shared borders, trading agreements, cultural links and kinship through intermarriage. These shared dimensions of experience supported friendly relations between clans in the confederacy.

Taungurung traditional land encompasses a large area of central Victoria, with clan estates bounded by natural topographic features such as river basins and mountain ranges, including the Broken, Delatite, Goulburn, Coliban and Campaspe watersheds:[5]

> We got one of the biggest areas in Victoria, the whole central part of Victoria from Kilmore, Benalla, Glenrowan, Beechworth, about 15 kilometres from Bright, back down over the Buffalo ranges, down along the Great Dividing Range back to Toolangi, Kinglake, Whittlesea, back to Kilmore. The top of the range is our boundary, the river can be the boundary too. The running rivers is where we get our strength from; the Goulburn River comes off the back of Mount Buller, the Acheron comes out of the back

---

2   Roy Patterson, in conversation with Jennifer Jones, 12 July 2016, DS300157.
3   Broome, *Aboriginal Victorians*, 186.
4   Smith et al., 'Fractional Identities', 542.
5   Clark, *Aboriginal Languages and Clans,* 370.

of Mount Donna Buang. Then you got the Rubicon and the Howqua rivers, near Molesworth; they all start up in the mountains and all come through my ancestral Country. The whole central part of Victoria and there is only nine clans in the whole area.[6]

The nine clans of the Taungurung people are organised into two kinship units, known as moieties, which have association with a special ancestor species or totem; Bunjil the Eaglehawk has five clans and Waa the Crow has four clans. Moiety affiliation influenced traditional marriage arrangements, land ownership and political authority.[7] Clan names are distinguished by two suffixes, 'balug' meaning a number of people and '(w)illam' meaning dwelling place.[8]

1. 'Buthera Balug' (Bunjil moiety) is associated with the Upper Goulburn near Yea and Seymour.

2. 'Look Willam' (Waa moiety) is associated with the Campaspe River near Kilmore.

3. 'Moomoom Gundidj' (Bunjil moiety) is associated with the area west of the Campaspe and north-west of Mitchelstown.

4. 'Nattarak Balug' (Waa moiety) is associated with the Coliban and Upper Campaspe rivers.

5. 'Nira Balug' (Waa moiety) adjoins Wurundjeri Country in the hills and valleys near Kilmore, Broadford, Pyalong and across towards Mount Macedon and Heathcote.

6. 'Warring-Illum Balug' (Bunjil moiety) is associated with the *Warring* or Upper Goulburn River at Yea and Alexandra.

7. 'Yarran Illam' (Bunjil moiety) is associated with land east of the Goulburn River below Seymour.

8. 'Yeerun-Illam-Balug' (Bunjil moiety) is associated with Benalla.

9. 'Yowung-Illam Balug' (Waa moiety) is associated with Alexandra, Mansfield and the Upper Goulburn.[9]

---

6   Roy Patterson, in conversation with Jennifer Jones, 15 April 2016, DS300142.
7   Barwick, 'Mapping the Past', 105.
8   Barwick, 'Mapping the Past', 106.
9   Clark, *Aboriginal Languages and Clans,* 369.

Five of these clan groups have descendants today. Each clan has spiritual and economic responsibilities for their estate. As Uncle Roy explains:

> Each clan was in a different area with their own information; we've got one mob here in this valley, we got another mob around Murchison. The southern side of Murchison is us; the northern side is Yorta Yorta. We got another mob up here at Mansfield, up into the mountain. There is a lot of area to cover, it is all mountain and river meeting in valleys. We travelled all around our Country. My family is from this area and up nearer to Wangaratta. My totem is the black crow. If anybody dies, he lets me know there's a death in the family. He comes over to where you are and goes 'arrk' and keeps on flyin'. It's just one 'arrk', nothing else, and he keeps on going. He is a beautiful bird. He is special to us, but to everyone else, he's a *bloody nuisance*![10]

Uncle Roy took inspiration from his totem, Waa, the crow. He was generous and funny, but he could also be fractious, contrary and outspoken. Uncle Roy argued, for example, that while his knowledge of bush tucker and bush medicine might hold some similarity with that of neighbouring Aboriginal groups, the cultural and geographical contexts are different:

> We are part of the Kulin Nation. All Aboriginals in this area of the Yarra Valley and that, Dandenong ranges and up all around here have got the same sort of tucker, but our culture is different. I had a bit of a barney with the shire about the cultural information they got from Wurundjeri people for an interpretive sign up here. I said, 'you've got no right to get that from Wurundjeri, you should have come to me, being Daunarung. This is Daunarung land and you've got no right to use other information. Our information is similar, but you've got no right to use their information on our ancestral Country'. Those signs had to be pulled down, and I gave them the information I had.[11]

Uncle Roy wanted to demonstrate that Taungurung history and culture is distinctive, because it has been shaped by particular people, experiences, beliefs and geographies.

---

10 Roy Patterson, in conversation with Jennifer Jones, 3 March 2016, DS3001137.
11 Roy Patterson, in conversation with Jennifer Jones, 3 March 2016, DS3001137.

Taungurung people and first contact

Before white invasion, Aboriginal life was shaped by responsibilities to land and by strategic coalitions and traditional enmity. Aboriginal nations outside the Kulin confederation were viewed as 'mainmait' or 'wild people' from far off Country.[12] Such pejorative terms indicated inferiority and untrustworthiness. Mainmait were blamed for unexplained deaths, for kidnapped women and for stolen resources. Foreign and distant clans were also held responsible when European diseases swept along Aboriginal trade routes between 1788 and 1829, before permanent white settlement in these southern districts.[13] Initial meetings with settlers on isolated pastoral runs were usually peaceful, as Europeans relied upon Aboriginal guides and traditional knowledge to find resources. As Uncle Roy suggests:

> When the white people first got here, they took one camp and the Aboriginal another, and they noticed what the Aboriginals were doing, so they did the same thing to get their food.[14]

Interracial conflict and violent reprisals became more frequent when Taungurung people understood that the Europeans intended to stay. Their disregard for Aboriginal culture led to conflict, often centred upon access to resources, or relating to kinship, reciprocity and respect for Country:[15]

> Cattle and sheep wanted to make camp at the waterhole, and there was a big fight over it, over the waterhole because white people reckoned it was theirs and the Aboriginal people reckoned it was theirs. If any animal come down to the water, they killed the animal. The white people shot the Aboriginals for killing their animals. We were classed as animals back then and are still being treated as animals by some people, even today.[16]

By the time Uncle Roy's great-grandmother Emma Kerr was born in 1853, punitive settler 'dispersals' had forced Aboriginal clans away from settled areas. First peoples congregated on or near protectorate stations established by government (1839–49) to access rations.[17] Here government officials

---

12 Clark, *Aboriginal Languages and Clans,* 418.
13 Campbell, *Invisible Invaders,* 152; Smith et al., 'Fractional Identities', 535.
14 Roy Patterson, in conversation with Jennifer Jones, 3 March 2016, DS3001137.
15 Broome, *Aboriginal Victorians*, 57.
16 Roy Patterson, in conversation with Jennifer Jones, 3 March 2016, DS3001137.
17 Protectorate stations were established in the Goulburn Valley, Loddon Valley, near Melbourne and in the Western District. See Barwick, 'Changes in the Aboriginal Population', 288.

induced them to assume civilised lifestyles and attempted to convert them to Christianity. Traditional differences and animosities between Aboriginal clans became less prominent in the later years of the protectorate, as numbers declined and customary lifestyles were difficult to practise.[18] Nevertheless, Aboriginal people made every effort to remain on their own Country for as long possible. Emma Kerr's mother, an unnamed Dja Dja Wurrung woman, gave birth to her daughter at Kelly's Station on Bendigo Creek. Emma Kerr's birthplace likely reflects the movement of Dja Dja Wurrung to the northern pastoral areas of their Country, in the wake of the gold rush.[19] Aboriginal workers could more easily gain employment on pastoral stations after white station hands joined the rush to Ballarat and Bendigo diggings. Officials estimated that, just after the rush, in 1853, Victoria was home to 80,000 settlers, 1,907 Aboriginal people and 6.5 million sheep.[20] An additional 500,000 settlers arrived during the first decade of the gold rush, and many stayed permanently. This increase in the white population forced the Victorian Government to develop new Aboriginal management policies. A Select Committee of the Legislative Council was appointed to enquire 'into the present condition of the Aborigines of this Colony' in 1858. Plans were devised to concentrate all First Nations groups in one isolated location, but William Thomas, Guardian of Aborigines, strongly advised against the measure. Drawing upon his understanding of attachment to Country, he advised that 'each tribe' should have 'a special place set apart on their own hunting ground'.[21] The Central Board Appointed to Watch Over the Interests of Aborigines (established as an outcome of this inquiry in 1859) initially heeded this advice. The Central Board subsequently oversaw the development of reserves across Victoria, including government-controlled stations and church-controlled missions.[22] One of the first stations was established on Taungurung land, at Acheron in the Upper Goulburn Valley, now known as Taggerty.[23] Uncle Roy's ancestors envisaged Acheron Aboriginal Station as a place where they could develop a self-sustaining agricultural enterprise while living on significant traditional land. Their hopes aligned with the stated priorities of government but, unfortunately, not with the ambitions of influential local squatters. The next chapter traces this clash of perspectives.

---

18   Clark, *Goulburn River Aboriginal Protectorate*, 91.
19   Broome, *Aboriginal Victorians*, 112; Attwood, *The Good Country*, 158.
20   Smith et al. 'Fractional Identities', 535.
21   William Thomas, minutes of evidence, 1 November 1858, in Victoria, Parliament, *Report of the Select Committee*.
22   Broome, *Aboriginal Victorians*, 126.
23   Noble, *The Red Gate*, 2.

2

Acheron Aboriginal Station: Land that 'ever should be theirs'

Uncle Roy's Taungurung ancestors were among the first Aboriginal people in southern Australia to negotiate the opening of a government station on their own land. Established in 1859, Acheron Aboriginal Station was named after the nearby waterway then known as the Nyaggeron, now Acheron River. Uncle Roy recalls the ancient associations between Taungurung people and this land:

> Back in the early days when the Europeans first came up here, my great-great-uncle Bandowick made a settlement down on the river opposite Cathedral Lane. The white people put them on a campsite there and said, 'you will be right here'. My ancestors had walked in this valley years ago, when the ground started to shake and rumble, and Nunnunthum started to come up out of Mother Earth to where it is today. When Europeans come into the valley, they saw this majestic peak and they said, 'that looks just like the spire of a Cathedral', so they called it Mount Cathedral. Its name is Nunnunthum.[1]

Uncle Roy's generational perspective highlights Taungurung peoples' deep knowledge of the land, including its true name. Spurred by this relationship, a deputation of Taungurung men approached Guardian of the Aborigines William Thomas on 28 February 1859 to secure this special

---

1   Roy Patterson, in conversation with Jennifer Jones, 15 April 2016, DS300142.

site. According to Thomas, Beaning, Murrin Murrin, Parugean, Baruppin and Koo-gurrin, and Wurundjeri translators Wonga and Munnarin, sought 'a particular part of the upper Goulburn, on the Acheron River to be set apart for them … to cultivate'.[2] Taungurung leaders, accompanied by Guardian Thomas and Assistant Surveyor Percy Bloomfield, then identified and marked out the desired site, south of the junction of the Acheron and Little rivers at the western foot of the Cathedral Range. Thomas recalled the jubilation of the Taungurung representatives upon their selection of a permanent refuge:

> The blacks chopped boundary trees, I sketched a chart of the country … 4500 acres more or less were surveyed with unlimited range to the NE, the blacks were perfectly satisfied in fact elated, [overjoyed at their success] as I passed thro' one and other group on my return wandering their way to the Promised Land. The blacks in these ranges are still a fine race wholesome in appearance, well accustomed to European labour, and ready to work and settle.[3]

Taungurung men marked boundary trees with the expectation that they had successfully claimed a place where they could work and settle. Although Taungurung people had been effectively 'removed from their country' by the end of 1839, they retained connections to Country by working for pastoralists.[4] Aboriginal people performed essential tasks that were 'unpopular with the white station hands' on Upper Goulburn Valley stations, including sheep washing, and were well acquainted with the demands of European farming.[5]

Of the two white men who witnessed the Taungurung mark out their chosen plot, only William Thomas appreciated that they deliberately claimed land suitable for agriculture, 'assuring me that "they would cultivate and set down on that land like white men"'.[6] Percy Bloomfield thought that Taungurung were not agriculturalists and would not select land with European crops in mind. He believed that Aboriginal land use was oriented towards hunting. Any reserve should, therefore, 'be acceptable

---

2   Mohican/Acheron Station January–June 1860, National Archives of Australia (hereafter NAA), B312, Item 2, Folio 7.
3   'Annual Report on Aborigines 1 January–31 December 1859', in Thomas, *Journal of William Thomas*, 248; journal entry, 18 March 1859, in Thomas, *Journal of William Thomas*, 196.
4   Kenny, 'Broken Treaty', 215.
5   Noble, *The Red Gate*, 6.
6   William Thomas, 'A History of the Settlement of the Blacks on the Upper Goulburn', 26 July 1860, Mohican/Acheron Station January–June 1860, NAA, B312, Item 2, Folio 7.

to the Aborigines [if] neither squatter or flocks [are] intervening between them and their hunting grounds'.[7] Bloomfield understood that most pastoral lands in Port Phillip had been claimed and occupied for decades, even in this isolated mountainous district. Local pastoralist Peter Snodgrass MLA recalled that, within two or three years of him 'taking up a station on the Muddy Creek [Yea River] and Goulburn River' in 1837–38, he was joined in the district by five additional squatters.[8] By 1840, 'there were runs all along the Goulburn … til the country became too mountainous for pastoralists'.[9] The proposed Acheron Aboriginal Station was not in unclaimed territory; it would excise 4,500 acres from two pastoral runs, the 16,000 acre Niagaroon and 50,000 acre Taggerty stations, respectively.[10]

The squatters who held these leases considered the country to be rightfully theirs and they responded decisively to the threat of Aboriginal repossession. Their actions drew upon mechanisms already developed to combat land reform legislation, using 'an elaborate machinery of deception involving highly skilled land sharks, agents and squatters'.[11] Squatters used these tactics to undermine and eventually preclude Aboriginal settlement in the Upper Goulburn district. Uncle Roy reflected on the efforts of his Taungurung ancestors and their dignified response when local squatters attempted to deprive them of their land at Acheron:

> So I'm proud of my great-great-great-uncle and the people working there, working with the white people and not letting them walk all over them. I'm not goin' to let them walk all over me neither. It is a beautiful thing to have pride and respect.[12]

As made evident below, the squatters who sought to dislodge Taungurung farmers from Acheron Station included men who had employed the same Aboriginal workers on their runs during the 1840s and 1850s. These squatters held respectable leadership positions in colonial society and purported to hold a benevolent interest in the fate of Taungurung people.

---

7   Mohican/Acheron Station 1859, NAA, B312, Item 1, Folio 16.
8   Bride, *Letters from Victorian Pioneers*, 215.
9   Bride, *Letters from Victorian Pioneers*, 216; Long, 'A History of Alexandra', 53.
10 See Billis and Kenyon, *Pastoral Pioneers*, 233, 256.
11 Legislation passed in September 1860. Powell, *The Public Lands of Australia Felix*, 76, 105.
12 Roy Patterson, in conversation with Jennifer Jones, 15 April 2016, DS3001141.

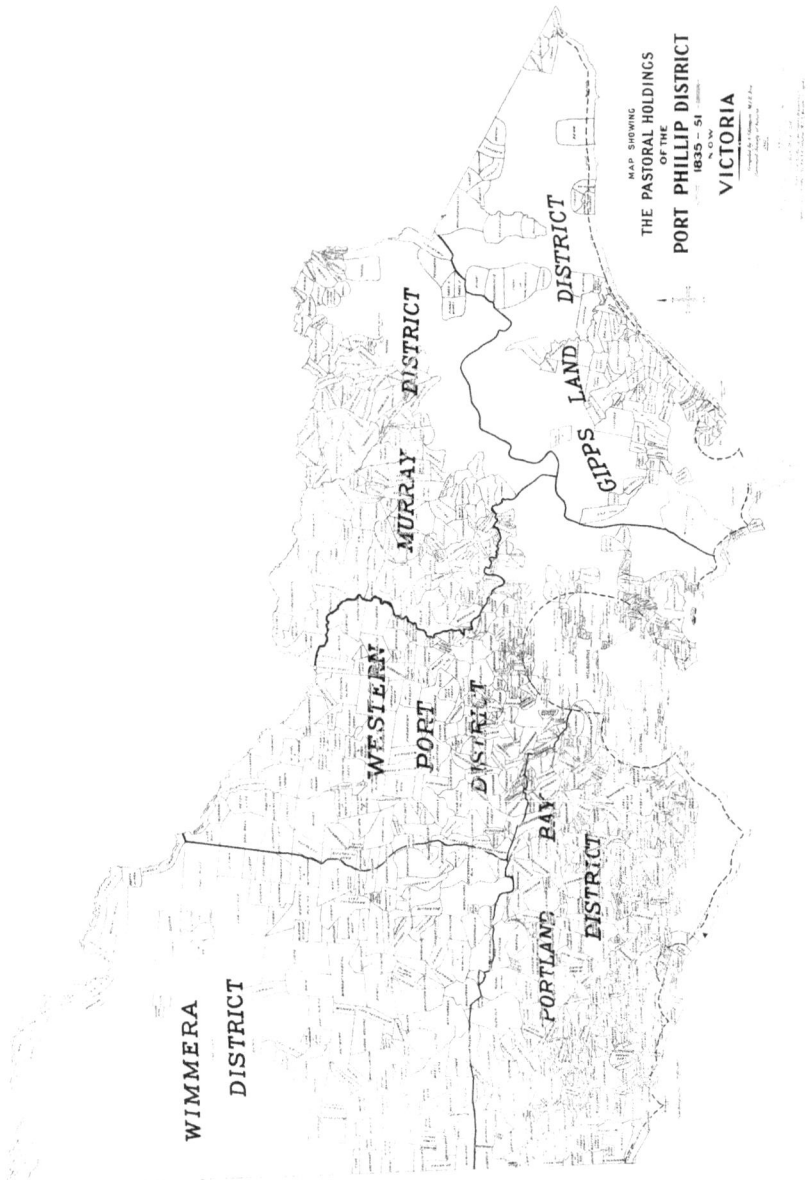

'Map showing the pastoral holdings of the Port Phillip District 1835–51, now Victoria'

Source: Billis and Keyon, *Pastoral Pioneers*, insert, back cover. Courtesy National Library of Australia, nla.gov.au/nla.obj-234157525/view.

Squatters disapprove of Acheron Aboriginal Station: Peter Snodgrass and the 'Goulburn Mob'

After the initial land rush in the Port Phillip District, squatters secured and expanded their holdings by working together as a self-interested bloc.[13] 'Old colonists' cooperated to control 'water sources, stock routes and information', making it difficult for newcomers to move into settled districts.[14] In the Upper Goulburn, a group of 'boisterous … hard riding, strong-headed young men, reckless horsemen, and gay sparks of young Melbourne', known collectively as the 'Goulburn Mob', cooperated to protect the prospects of their set. Together they took action to deter 'conscientious officials' like William Thomas who were working in the interests of Traditional Owners.[15]

The land selected by Taungurung leaders fell within the 'pre-emptive right' of Henry Johnson, who held Taggerty Station from 1849 to 1864.[16] Under regulations gazetted in 1848, a pre-emptive right allowed squatters to purchase a homestead block of 640 acres within their leasehold, before the 'land in their locality was made available to the general public'.[17] Given these entitlements, and the widely held view that the pre-emptive section of Taggerty would be 'depreciated in value by the establishment of the proposed Aboriginal Reserve', officials expected that Henry Johnson would object to the Taungurung selection.[18] This was the case. In January 1860, District Surveyor F. Pinnifer reported to the commissioner of lands that 'the present owner of Taggerty <u>does</u> object to being surrounded by an Aboriginal reserve and seems to consider the present survey a hardship upon him'.[19] Pinnifer further reported a 'general feeling amongst the squatters averse to the proximity to an Aboriginal reserve', reasoning that 'the Aborigines keeping to and fro and hunting about with their dogs must

---

13   Boyce, *1835*, 155.
14   Boyce, *1835*, 155.
15   Bride, *Letters from Victorian Pioneers*, 215; Boyce, *1835*, 154.
16   Mohican/Acheron Station 1859, NAA, B312, Item 1, Folio 16.
17   'Pre-Emptive Rights (1852–1873)' in *VPRS 8168 Historic Plan Collection*, accessed 16 January 2018, wiki.prov.vic.gov.au/index.php/VPRS_8168_Historic_Plan_Collection#PR_PRE-EMPTIVE_RIGHTS_.281852_-_1873.29; Billis and Kenyon, *Pastoral Pioneers*, 256.
18   Mohican/Acheron Station 1859, NAA, B312, Item 1, Folio 16.
19   F. Pinnifer to the Hon Commissioner of Lands and Survey, 12 January 1860, Acheron Station January–June 1860, NAA, B312, Item 2, Folios 3–1A (original emphasis).

be an annoyance to the owners of either cattle or sheep running at large'.[20] Vehement squatter disapproval was communicated to the Central Board Appointed to Watch Over the Interests of Aborigines via a campaign of letters from June 1859. These letters included objections from influential pastoral entrepreneur Hugh Glass, a leaseholder of Niagaroon Station since 1850.[21] Claiming serious loss and inconvenience, Glass wrote to the honorary secretary, Central Board, requesting:

> Will you be good enough to inform me if it is the intention of the Board to retain possession for an Aboriginal reserve of the portion of my licenced run known as the Niagaroon … which is at present so used. The Superintendent [of Acheron Aboriginal Station] informs me he has no orders to remove and is at present planting potatoes on the ground—the want of this portion of my run is a very serious loss and inconvenience to me at the present time.[22]

One of the richest men in Australia in the late 1850s, and the wealthiest man in Victoria in 1862, Hugh Glass had a voracious appetite for land. He acquired and traded 49 runs in Victoria from 1840 to 1869, and was understood to have 'dummied, cheated and bribed to gain his own ends'.[23] Glass was also known as a charming, generous and humane man—except when his intentions were thwarted. To protect his interests, Glass and his associates manipulated public officials and influenced politicians in the Legislative Assembly.[24] One of these politicians was Peter Snodgrass, a member of the 'Goulburn Mob'. The son of a soldier and colonial administrator, Peter Snodgrass was 21 when he began squatting in the Upper Goulburn Valley.[25] He soon gained a reputation for 'dissipating all the money that his father had supplied him with', but he was also known to be 'shrewd, steady and well loved by all'.[26] To win over his prospective father-in-law, John Cotton, in 1846, Snodgrass promised to 'reform his habits and become more steady'.[27] Cotton accepted Snodgrass's remorse as genuine and noted:

20   F. Pinnifer to the Hon Commissioner of Lands and Survey, 12 January 1860, Acheron Station January–June 1860, NAA, B312, Item 2, Folios 3–1A.
21   Billis and Kenyon, *Pastoral Pioneers*, 58, 233; Kiddle, *Men of Yesterday*.
22   Hugh Glass to R. Brough Smythe Honorary Secretary to Central Aboriginal Board, 12 September 1860, Mohican/Acheron Station January–June 1860, NAA, B312, Item 2, Folio 24.
23   Kiddle, *Men of Yesterday*, 262.
24   de Serville, *Pounds and Pedigrees*, 99.
25   Lea-Scarlett, 'Snodgrass, Kenneth (1784–1853)', *Australian Dictionary of Biography*, accessed online 15 January 2019, adb.anu.edu.au/biography/snodgrass-kenneth-2675/text3737.
26   John Cotton to William Cotton, 6 March 1846, in Mackaness, *The Correspondence of John Cotton*, 33.
27   John Cotton to William Cotton, 6 March 1846, in Mackaness, *The Correspondence of John Cotton*, 33.

> Mr Snodgrass has been a spendthrift, and is now, I am sorry to
> say, obliged to live with me, having no property of his own. He is,
> however, hardworking and remarkably good tempered, kind to
> Agnes, and disposed to act the part of overseer for me.[28]

Acting as station manager at Doogallook, Snodgrass proved his worth by
controlling an outbreak of catarrh, a virulent respiratory infection that
devastated Cotton's flocks in 1848.[29] Although 5,000 sheep died and Cotton
sustained a loss 'equal to £1300', he noted that the business would 'have
been in a mess' without the 'valuable assistance' of his son-in-law. Cotton
later apprenticed his eldest son William to Snodgrass, noting his 'good head
[and] foresight'.[30] This management role at Doogallook continued after John
Cotton's sudden death in December 1849. Snodgrass became co-owner
of Doogallook after the death of his mother-in-law, Susannah Cotton, in
1852. By this time, Snodgrass was also an elected political representative
for the district. He therefore had significant personal financial interests and
political influence in the Upper Goulburn when his neighbours objected
to the creation of an Aboriginal reserve in the vicinity, including, later, sole
ownership of Doogallook Station (1860–65).[31]

A liberal by political persuasion, Snodgrass was elected to the first Victorian
Legislative Council in 1851. Here he was soon known as a supporter of
squatter interests.[32] He later represented two electorates encompassing
the Upper Goulburn in the Victorian Legislative Assembly, from 1856 to
1867. At this time, the parliament was polarised between the conservative
right and democratic left, which, according to Geoffrey Serle, enabled
'liberals, opportunists and eccentrics' like Snodgrass to occupy the centre
ground. Here, 'their whims and prejudices were to rule governments'.[33]

Unfortunately for Snodgrass, such popularity and privilege did not
guarantee financial success. Economic difficulties may have opened
him to the suite of corrupt practices that were aired after his death in
1867.[34] It was his renown as an upstanding local squatter, however, that

---

28   John Cotton to William Cotton, June 1848, in Mackaness, *The Correspondence of John Cotton*, 17.
29   Mylrea, 'Catarrh in Sheep', 298. The outbreak was compounded by low prices, high wages and footrot.
30   John Cotton to William Cotton, February 1849 in Mackaness, *The Correspondence of John Cotton*, 37.
31   Billis and Kenyon, *Pastoral Pioneers*, 137.
32   Serle, *The Golden Age*, 259.
33   Serle, *The Golden Age*, 259.
34   Glass named Snodgrass as his corrupt agent to a select committee in 1869, see Kiddle, *Men of Yesterday*, 251; de Serville, *Pounds and Pedigrees*, 99.

prompted Guardian of Aborigines William Thomas to recommend Snodgrass as trustee for Acheron Aboriginal Station.[35] Thomas wrote to the Central Board on 12 April 1859 recommending Snodgrass to oversee the Aboriginal settlement, along with John Maxwell of Cathkin.[36] Fellow trustees included John Christie Aitken of Thornton and Acheron, runs that adjoined the Aboriginal station,[37] and Donald Mackenzie of Mt Pleasant.[38] Thomas commented that 'the neighbouring gentlemen are highly respectable and for years have been … much interested in the blacks'.[39] Thomas also recommended that Robert Hickson 'have charge of the Aboriginal establishment' and, on 15 April 1859, Hickson was appointed superintendent.[40] Like the new trustees, Hickson also claimed an association with, and interest in, Aboriginal people. This regard was apparently reciprocated as 'two of the Goulburn Blacks' hearing that 'Mr Hickson will have charge over the Station' were reportedly 'pleased [and] say he is a good man they know him long time'.[41] As discussed below (and in further detail in Chapter 3), Hickson and Snodgrass were both drawn from the small circle of elite Upper Goulburn settler society. These gentlemen, however, held competing aims for the new Aboriginal reserve. Their opposing views led to their public estrangement and, eventually, to the forced removal of Taungurung people from their own Country.

Peter Snodgrass agreed to act as a local trustee for Acheron Aboriginal Station, a position of trust and responsibility for the benefit of Taungurung people, on 1 June 1859. His loyalties, however, seem never to have focused on Aboriginal interests or perspectives. Snodgrass was instead acting with fellow pastoralists to remove Taungurung people from their selected land as quickly as possible. Snodgrass first campaigned for relocation of the settlement to the less desirable and more remote Mohican Station in alliance with owner and fellow parliamentarian James Stewart MLC

---

35   Thomas received this letter of acceptance on 1 June 1859 and the position was approved 13 June 1860. 'Annual Report to the Central Board January 1861', in Thomas, *Journal of William Thomas*, 213, 319–21; Mohican/Acheron Station 1859, NAA, B312, Item 1, Folio 16.

36   This 20,480-acre station was jointly owned with Hugh Glass from 1851–59, and by Maxwell alone from 1859–64. Billis and Kenyon, *Pastoral Pioneers*, 168.

37   'Thornton', 24,000 acres near Yea, Billis and Kenyon, *Pastoral Pioneers*, 3.

38   'Acheron', 19,200 acres adjoining the Aboriginal station, Billis and Kenyon, *Pastoral Pioneers*, 89.

39   William Thomas to Central Board, 12 April 1859, Mohican/Acheron Station 1859, NAA, B312, Item 1, Folio 12.

40   Journal entry, 30 March and 15 April 1859, in Thomas, *Journal of William Thomas*, 201, 204.

41   Journal entry, 30 March and 15 April 1859, in Thomas, *Journal of William Thomas*, 201, 204.

(member for the Eastern Province 1856–63).[42] Snodgrass also assisted the former owner of Mohican Station, Stephen Beever Jones, to claim financial compensation for stock losses attributed to the proximity of the Aboriginal reserve at Acheron. These actions were personally motivated, as Snodgrass needed to recoup monies owed to him by Stephen Beever Jones. As Guardian William Thomas was to bemoan, Aboriginal ambition at Acheron was 'defeated … because [of] a needy broken down squatter'.[43] Oral knowledge handed down to Uncle Roy Patterson provides an overview:

> The white people got greedy and said, 'we will put you in a new area', so they shunted them up to the head of the Rubicon where they thought it was too rocky. They took them up Cathedral Lane, up to the Rubicon and put them on a campsite there.[44]

'Because [of] a needy broken down squatter'

Although Mohican Station was adjacent to the station Taungurung people had selected to cultivate and settle at Acheron, it was contrasting in terms of amenity. A 16,000-acre tract of land with frontage on the same river, Mohican was 'much higher and colder' than Acheron. According to Superintendent Robert Hickson, the country was deficient, as it was 'full of game' that competed with the stock. The run had 'only a small patch of good land' suitable for agriculture and 'the Blacks hated it'.[45]

When Mohican Station was first occupied by white settlers in May 1851, the run was reported to have 'sufficient grazing capabilities for 5000 sheep'.[46] The executors of John Cotton's estate (his widow Suzannah and son-in-law Charles Ryan) purchased the licence in 1851 and held it until 1855, with only 80 head of 'quiet cattle'. When it was advertised for sale in July 1855, the executors claimed that Mohican had a carrying capacity

---

42   John Cotton's wife Susannah and his son-in-law Charles Ryan were executors of the estate. Susannah Cotton died in 1852. 'John COTTON', Probate and Administration Files, Public Record Office Victoria (hereafter PROV), VPRS 28/P0, Unit 4, Item A/304.

43   'For Report June 1863', William Thomas Papers, 1834–1868, Mitchell Library (hereafter ML), MSS 214/19, Frame 117.

44   Roy Patterson, in conversation with Jennifer Jones, 15 April 2016, DS300141.

45   Minutes of the Special Meeting of the Central Board for Aborigines, 3 May 1861, NAA, B314, Roll 1.

46   'Government Notices', *Geelong Advertiser*, 5 May 1851, 3.

of '800–1000 head' of cattle.[47] Potential buyers were right to be sceptical. Colonial knowledge of the time had it that 'most of the best land was taken up before the end of the [eighteen] thirties, and what remained appeared to offer poorer yields and higher costs, especially for transport'.[48] Located in a cold and isolated mountain district that early squatters had spurned, Mohican Station was assessed by District Surveyor F. Pinnifer in 1860 as so poor that 'no European person would care to occupy it'; as for the stock, it was 'not worth mustering'.[49] The owners of such unproductive tracts relied upon the unschooled optimism of inexperienced or monied new arrivals to relieve them of such lands.

Stephen Beever Jones was apparently such a man. He purchased Mohican Station from the executors of John Cotton's estate with some confidence in 1855. This optimism was reflected in his decision to try sheep, although they were untested on the run. Beever Jones bought 1,000 sheep for an outlay of £400, presumably on terms that later ruined him.[50] Securing sheep for new stations was costly in this period, and available sheep were also renowned for their low quality. This was because an established pastoralist who could carry more sheep on his own lands 'would only sell his worst'.[51] As Abbott noted, the 'fortunes of sheep farming were more the product of sales of sheep than wool' and relied upon 'attracting monied immigrants to purchase some of this increase'.[52] John Cotton had disposed of stock and station in this advantageous manner in 1844, selling his property on the Devils River to a Mr Matson. Cotton noted privately that he resolved to 'sell the station as the sheep have not done well there' but did this advantageously, selling them for 10/- each when he had purchased the same sheep at 4/6 per head.[53] It is perhaps unsurprising that, 'having incurred a heavy debt' to buy the sheep, Matson was forced to relinquish 'the station with all the sheep, cattle and everything on the run' to cover the debt in February 1849.[54] It was then common for settlers to obtain 'necessary advances which [were] from

---

47   'Stations and Livestock for Sale', *The Argus*, 13 July 1855, 8.
48   Butlin, *Foundations of the Australian Monetary System*, 317.
49   F. Pinnifer to Commissioner of Lands and Survey, 12 January 1860, Mohican/Acheron Station January–June 1860, NAA, B312, Item 2, Folios 3–1A.
50   F. Pinnifer to Commissioner of Lands and Survey, 12 January 1860, Mohican/Acheron Station January–June 1860, NAA, B312, Item 2, Folios 3–1A.
51   Butlin, *Foundations of the Australian Monetary System*, 317.
52   Abbott, *The Pastoral Age*, 124–25.
53   John Cotton to William Cotton, 6 March 1846, in Mackaness, *The Correspondence of John Cotton*, 33.
54   John Cotton to William Cotton, 6 March 1846, in Mackaness, *The Correspondence of John Cotton*, 33.

time to time required' to maintain their pastoral activities. Many found themselves thus ruined: '[in] arrears to pay up on the purchase of their stock, and to meet their engagements they had no alternative but to sell at a ruinous sacrifice'.[55]

Guardian of Aborigines William Thomas understood that Stephen Beever Jones had become indebted in this manner when he purchased Mohican Station. Thomas noted that Aboriginal hopes for Acheron had been:

> Defeated after all because a needy broken down squatter owed £800 to 2 merchants I believe one in upper house and one in the lower transferred. His station was bought by Stewart.[56]

Those merchants, James Stewart and Peter Snodgrass, had direct interests in the Mohican run when they recognised an opportunity to benefit their personal financial positions. They did this by influencing a government agency to acquire the property for the use of Aboriginal people from the hapless Stephen Beever Jones.

Little is known about Stephen Beever Jones prior to his purchase of Mohican Station.[57] He was born in Yorkshire in 1808, the son of gamekeeper John Beever and Martha Littlewood. He was resident in Buninyong, a major inland community of pre–gold rush Victoria, and Melbourne for the births of his first three children between 1845 and 1852.[58] Beever Jones moved to the Upper Goulburn when he purchased Mohican Station. Just nine months later, he sold the barren run to hoteliers and land speculators John Brown and James Stewart.

Beever Jones also apparently remained indebted to Snodgrass after the transaction, perhaps relating to the sale of sheep.[59] Vacating Mohican in 1859, Beever Jones moved to nearby Upper Thornton and into the hotel trade. His bark-roofed shanty at Upper Thornton was known as the Full Belly Hotel in 1862, metamorphosising into the more decorous Old House at Home and, later, perhaps reflecting long-waited financial success and respectability, the Harvest Home.[60] Brown and Stewart

---

55 Kerr, *Glimpses of Life in Victoria*, 49.
56 'For Report June 1863', William Thomas Papers, 1834–1868, ML, MSS 214/19, Frame 117.
57 Including when or why he chose to adopt the surname Jones.
58 Lloyd, *Alexandra and District*, 279.
59 Billis and Kenyon, *Pastoral Pioneers*, 218.
60 Lloyd *Alexandra and District*, 279.

had apparently known Beever Jones for 'many years', possibly indicating a previous occupation in the liquor trade and a connection between the men in the vicinity of Ballarat.[61]

Wine merchant James Stewart diversified into pastoral holdings after the success of his hotel business with partner John 'Como' Brown, which included lucrative wayside inns.[62] James Stewart represented Victoria's Eastern Province in the Legislative Council from November 1856 to August 1863.[63] Soon after Brown and Stewart purchased the valueless Mohican Station, they sought to immediately onsell the run at a profit.

Brown and Stewart tendered Mohican Station as suitable for Aboriginal settlement in early 1859, offering the property to the government for £1,500. As Diane Barwick noted, Brown and Stewart were essentially asking the government to purchase leased Crown Land at considerable cost.[64] The businessmen nominated Peter Snodgrass as their agent, noting that 'for locality we beg to refer you to P Snodgrass Esq who is well acquainted with the same and can give you all the necessary information'.[65] Snodgrass was very well acquainted with the property, as he managed the Cotton family business that had held the lease for four years. It is difficult to ascertain to what extent these parliamentarians influenced the decision of the Central Board to buy the licence but, at their next meeting, the Board recommended 'the advisableness of purchasing the stock and goodwill of a station in the use of aborigines'.[66] Guardian William Thomas expected this decision to secure the land that Taungurung leaders had selected at Acheron. He had, therefore, authorised the foundation of the settlement in advance. Trustee Peter Snodgrass and his squatting allies had other ideas.

Recognising that more pressure might help secure the sale of Mohican, Brown and Stewart wrote to the commissioner of lands and survey to make claims of injury caused by Aboriginal farmers. They cited a letter from Stephen Beever Jones who claimed that his stock had been killed by marauding dogs:

---

61   Brown and Stewart to C. W. Ligar, Surveyor-General, 16 May 1859, Mohican/Acheron Station 1859, NAA, B312, Item 1, Folio 2.
62   Brown was already a noted builder in 1840s boomtown Melbourne. See 'HO10 – Rockbank Inn', *Victorian Heritage Database*, accessed 19 January 2018, vhd.heritagecouncil.vic.gov.au/places/162932.
63   James Stewart in 'Re-Member Database', *Parliament of Victoria*, accessed 19 January 2018, www.parliament.vic.gov.au/about/people-in-parliament/re-member/details/24/1000.
64   Barwick, *Rebellion at Coranderrk*, 47.
65   Brown and Stewart to C. W. Ligar, Surveyor-General, 16 May 1859, Mohican/Acheron Station 1859, NAA, B312, Item 1, Folio 2.
66   23 May 1859, Mohican/Acheron Station 1859, NAA, B312, Item 1, Folio 4.

We are in receipt of a letter from Mr Jones (who is in charge of the station) … This person is hard working, industrious and has been known to us many years and should the aborigines continue in the neighbourhood the prosperity of the station will be so much injured as to completely ruin him. It being much apparent that the locality is a most suitable one as an aboriginal reserve, [we] are here respectfully to call your attention to any offer for selling it.[67]

Beever Jones had alerted Brown and Stewart to the perilous 'state of this station owing to the close proximity of the blacks'. He claimed:

I am in a fair way of losing all my sheep their dogs killing them in all directions and driving them into the scrub even destroying them in the yard at night. They have committed such havoc among them that I am scarcely able to muster 300 sheep. I had 9 rams in my paddock 8 of which they have killed by flushing them into the river. There are 66 blackfellows at the protectorate and each one possessing not less than 5 or 6 dogs. So you can imagine gentlemen how delightfully I am situated with my unfortunate sheep.[68]

The misfortunes of Stephen Beever Jones, and the fate of his sheep, were well known in the Upper Goulburn. Reliable local informants told District Surveyor Pinnifer that Jones's failure predated this claimed injury of 26 June 1859. His hardship had nothing to do with the Aboriginal settlement on Acheron:

Stephen Jones' complaint of injury to his sheep by aboriginal dogs … seems to be much exaggerated. Prior to the establishment of the Aboriginal Station, his sheep were in a very bad and diseased state and his misfortunes are probably due more to the unsuitability of the country and other causes … I am credibly informed that originally (three or four years ago) when sheep were first tried on the station, Jones purchased one thousand sheep for £400, but nobody seems to know what has become of them.[69]

---

67   Brown and Stewart to Commissioner of Lands and Survey, 14 July 1859, Mohican/Acheron Station 1859, NAA, B312, Item 1, Folio 4.
68   Letter, Stephen Jones to Brown and Stewart, 26 June 1859, Mohican/Acheron Station 1859, NAA, B312, Item 1, Folio 6.
69   F. Pinnifer to Commissioner of Lands and Survey, 12 January 1860, Mohican/Acheron Station January–June 1860, NAA, B312, Item 2, Folios 3–1A.

Jones was now claiming £1,000 compensation for the loss of sheep that had cost £400—a cost attributed to his poor management and the unsuitability of the location.[70] As noted earlier, stock diseases associated with wet weather, including catarrh, had caused significant losses across the district, meaning 'the end of most squatters, since stock represented almost all their assets'.[71]

Taungurung disappointment: The Central Board concedes to squatter demands

Whether Jones's sheep died because of dog attack or disease, it is apparent that Brown, Stewart and Snodgrass went to some effort to ensure that Mohican was purchased for the Upper Goulburn Aboriginal settlement instead of the site selected by Taungurung leaders. This aim was achieved at the first meeting of the Central Board, 8 June 1860, when a resolution was passed:

> That the Board affirm the desirability of possessing the Mohican Station improvements and stock and land for the purposes of an Aboriginal reserve and recommend that an arrangement be made with Mr Jones and his agents as to the purchase.[72]

Brown and Stewart succeeded in selling the station, but not in claiming additional compensation for Stephen Beever Jones.[73] On 2 May 1860, Guardian of Aborigines William Thomas protested the claimed compensation of £1,000 as excessive, arguing that the entire station could be secured for that sum, and still represent handsome compensation for any harm.[74] Thomas, however, had also assumed that the Central Board would purchase Mohican Station in addition to the selected land at Acheron. He did not envisage the relocation of the Aboriginal settlement to this more isolated and less conducive location, or the removal of Taungurung people from culturally meaningful land.

---

70   Brown and Stewart to E. Hodginson, Deputy Surveyor, 23 June 1860, Mohican/Acheron Station January–June 1860, NAA, B312, Item 2, Folio 30.
71   Noble, *The Red Gate*, 8. The district was one of the last in Victoria to eradicate scab, in 1876.
72   Mohican/Acheron Station January–June 1860, NAA, B312, Item 2, Folio 15.
73   Brown and Stewart to E. Hodginson, Deputy Surveyor, 23 June 1860, Mohican/Acheron Station January–June 1860, NAA, B312, Item 2, Folio 30.
74   William Thomas to Central Board, 2 May 1860, Mohican/Acheron Station January–June 1860, NAA, B312, Item 2, Folio 12.

William Thomas had authorised and inaugurated the Aboriginal reserve at Acheron under the expectation that necessary funds would be allocated to support the farming venture. He was, therefore, surprised on Sunday 10 July 1859 when a deputation of three disappointed Taungurung men, Nartal, Bunnemuttera and Burrawein, protested that their agricultural enterprise needed supplies.[75] The trio had travelled to Melbourne with a bullock team to collect a requisition of agricultural implements, and were 'very cut up' when they were denied permission by the colonial storekeeper. Thomas made 'the best excuse I can', as he believed the requisition had been approved.[76] He wrote to the commissioner of lands and surveys noting:

> The unfortunate position of the Upper Goulburn Aboriginal Settlement recently formed, (thro' want of funds) and the lamentable failure likely to result in consequence, the disappointment of a body of intelligent and industrious Aborigines, who have congregated there inured to civilised labor to settle down on their own soil, is a disappointment I never anticipated to have to write upon.[77]

The requisition had not been honoured in early January 1860. Thomas argued that he had 'made out a requisition consisting of bullocks, dray, agricultural implements &C&C which was at once sanctioned by government', yet 'there was no funds to meet the requisition tho approved of'.[78] Thomas was nevertheless optimistic: 'notwithstanding the loss of time, I have no doubt but these industrious mountaineer blacks will shortly make a shew upon the station'.[79] Thomas had overseen 'a grand opening' of the settlement on August 1859, with 'no less than 107 from 4 Mountainous Tribes' in residence. Despite this 'promising opening', provision had not been made to support the settlement.[80]

---

75 Journal entry, 10 July 1859, in Thomas, *Journal of William Thomas*, 218.

76 'Annual Report on Aborigines 1 January–31 December 1859, in Thomas, *Journal of William Thomas*, 248.

77 Guardian of Aborigines to Honourable Commissioner of Lands and Surveys, 'Proposing a plan to provide support of the Aborigines throughout the Colony of Victoria', 20 July 1859, transcribed by Pauline Byrt, in Thomas, *Journal of William Thomas*, 220–21.

78 Thomas, *Journal of William Thomas*, 220–21; William Thomas, 'A History of the Settlement of the Blacks on the Upper Goulburn', 26 July 1860, Mohican/Acheron Station January–June 1860, NAA, B312, Item 2, Folio 7.

79 'Annual Report on Aborigines 1 January–31 December 1859', in Thomas, *Journal of William Thomas*, 248.

80 'Annual Report on Aborigines 1 January–31 December 1859', in Thomas, *Journal of William Thomas*, 248.

Acheron Aboriginal Station had been surveyed and opened in 1859 with much optimism, but prospects for permanent settlement soon deteriorated. The land claimed by Taungurung leaders had not been officially gazetted, and now the treasurer refused to allocate funds based on a supplementary estimate.[81] Attempts by Snodgrass to relocate the settlement were well underway by February 1860, when William Thomas somehow secured money to purchase tools and supplies. Unaware of these undermining efforts, Taungurung farmers prepared for cropping between February and June 1860. William Thomas reported their progress on 29 August 1860:

> Work done included cutting logs for and erecting 4-rail cultivation paddock fence, grubbing trees from the 15 acre cultivation paddock ... stripped bark for a store ... grubbing and cleaning ground for wheat, stripping bark and building their own winter mia mia's ... ploughed, sewed and farrowed five acres of wheat, fenced about one and a half acres of land for a garden, ploughed and layed out beds, walks, sewing the vegetable seeds, raking and cleansing the walks of grass.[82]

Taungurung farmers also prepared 10 acres for potatoes and, taking 'a more lively interest in the progress of the establishment, are well contented with the place and more settled than they have hitherto been'.[83] Just 12 days after this high level of Taungurung industry was noted, two community representatives arrived in Melbourne 'much alarmed at being told [they] must leave Acheron station'. Trustee Peter Snodgrass had ordered the removal of staff and stores 'from the Acheron River to the Mohican station'.[84] Taungurung leaders met Thomas again on 30 August, protesting the order to relocate and 'again plead[ing]' for justice:[85]

> The blacks were dissatisfied so much so that they persisted in not [offering] the least assistance in removing the stores—the objection of the natives appears to be dependent on it not being the spot they selected <u>that it will be injurious to their health</u> ... It would appear that on the superintendent and his wife leaving for

81 Christie, *Aborigines in Colonial Victoria*, 158.
82 'Returns of the Acheron Aboriginal Establishment Report for Period 1 January 1860 to 3 June 1860', Mohican/Acheron Station June–December 1860, NAA, B312, Item 3, Folios 21–21A.
83 Mohican/Acheron Station June–December 1860, NAA, B312, Item 3, Folios 21–21A.
84 Journal entry, 29 August 1860, Thomas, *Journal of William Thomas*, 277; 'Returns from the Superintendent of the Acheron Aboriginal Reserve for the Quarter Ending the 30 September 1860', Mohican/Acheron Station June–December 1860, NAA, B312, Item 3, Folio 28.
85 Journal entry, 30 August 1860, in Thomas, *Journal of William Thomas*, 278.

good their selected spot on the 19th September that the blacks to the number of forty eight left in a body, leaving [a] few lubras to accompany the superintendent, even refusing to remain to take care of the crops they had sown.[86]

According to Robert Hickson, 'the belief that Messrs Glass and Nash were to take possession of the portion of the station … frequented by the blacks' was enough to prompt the Taungurung to abandon the improvements they had made.[87] Diane Barwick argued that Hugh Glass was a ruthless man who 'had cheated Bunurong and Wurundjeri employees' and that the Kulin were wise to avoid his displeasure.[88] Oral history handed down to Uncle Roy Patterson suggests that the squatters objected to Aboriginal use of pastoral land for agriculture. Conditions of their own licences restricted the use of land to 'depasturing purposes only', and squatters feared agricultural development of the district by land-hungry gold-seekers, as eventuated after 1865.[89] Uncle Roy recalls:

> When more white people came up there and started mining gold, they saw the Aboriginal people growing good food. They had thought it was too rocky up there, but it was obviously good land. Then the squatters got greedy and said 'we will put you in a new area', so they shunted the Daunarung up to the head of the Rubicon and took over the Black ground again.[90]

Snodgrass and his colleagues succeeded in evicting Taungurung farmers from their land in September 1860. In the same month, Victorian squatters conceded their first loss in a larger struggle: to prevent the passage of land reform legislation into law. After months of obstruction by squatting interests in the Legislative Council, the *Sale of Crown Lands Act* (known as the Nicholson Act) was finally passed in September 1860. The Bill, which aimed to extend small-scale farming and intensive cultivation into new districts, was strenuously opposed by a 'clique of mighty squatters' in the Legislative Council, including James Stewart. Although these men held 'large portions of this very soil, at less than one farthing per acre', they worked strenuously to prevent the sale of 'small lots to industrious men at

---

86   William Thomas to Central Board, 10 November 1860, Mohican/Acheron Station June–December 1860, NAA, B312, Item 3, Folio 41 (original emphasis).
87   Robert Hickson, report to Peter Snodgrass Esq., 5 Dec 1860, Mohican/Acheron Station June–December 1860, NAA, B312, Item 3, Folios 46A–49.
88   Barwick, *Rebellion at Coranderrk*, 34.
89   Noble, *The Red Gate*, 23.
90   Roy Patterson, in conversation with Jennifer Jones, 3 March 2016, DS3001137.

eighty-fold the price they pay'.[91] Government had particularly targeted areas around the central Victorian goldfields for closer settlement, as the alluvial phase of the gold rush was in decline and miners were seeking new and autonomous occupations.[92] The success of Aboriginal farmers at Acheron coincided unhappily with the passage of this land reform Bill, and with increased pressure for land selection that accompanied mining activity in the Upper Goulburn. Crown Land in the district had been judged by the surveyor-general to be poor-to-average in quality, and hence more suited to livestock than intense cultivation, but local smallholders were nevertheless increasing cereal cropping to meet market demand.[93] Agriculture in the central district rose 9.4 per cent between 1860 and 1862, primarily for food crops wheat, oats and hay.[94] A successful harvest by Aboriginal people, who were widely assumed to be inferior to white people in almost all realms of activity, would openly demonstrate the agricultural potential of local landholdings. The first actions of squatters Glass and Nash, after the eviction of the Aboriginal farmers, was, therefore, to destroy the four-rail fence erected to protect crops in the cultivation paddock. Guardian William Thomas narrated the destruction:

> It would appear that Messrs' Glass and Nash have taken possession of the reserve originally selected by the Aborigines ... and that the superintendent has been ordered by them to remove the government bullock on the 13th ... and by the 17th the cultivation fence on the reserve had been broken down and the crop of wheat and potatoes destroyed. This the fate of Aboriginal industry is enough to deter Aborigines from ever after having confidence in promises held out to them.[95]

Thomas also reported to the Central Board that 'the blackfellows were so disgusted and disappointed leaving the reserve and all they had done' that the superintendent:

> Could not get one of the blacks to drive the dray with the stores to the Mohican station that he was forced to drive the dray himself, that the blacks refused to come to live on the Mohican station.[96]

---

91   John Fawkner to the editor, 'The Obstructive Sixteen', *The Age*, 31 May 1860, 5. Mohican/Acheron Station January–June 1860, NAA, B312, Item 2, Folio 15.
92   Attempts to achieve this outcome in the Western District was a controversial failure. Powell, *The Public Lands of Australia Felix*, 86; Serle, *The Golden Age*. 287.
93   This assessment related to Kilmore district. Powell, *The Public Lands of Australia Felix*, 87.
94   Powell, *The Public Lands of Australia Felix*, 87.
95   William Thomas to Central Board, 22 November 1860, Mohican/Acheron Station June–December 1860, NAA, B312, Item 3, Folio 44.
96   William Thomas to Central Board, 8 October 1860, Mohican/Acheron Station June–December 1860, NAA, B312, Item 3, Folio 33.

Superintendent Hickson not only had to drive the bullock himself, but also discovered there was no yard to hold the beast at the new site 'in consequence of the fencing being all decayed'.[97] The contrasting quality of land is identifiable on surveyor maps, as the soil at Acheron was noted to be 'alluvial flat timbered with gum', while Jones's Mohican Station was dominated by 'sandstone ranges' and 'soil of medium quality very broken and heavily timbered'.[98] Little wonder the Taungurung farmers were so 'disgusted and disappointed'. In his bitter criticism of the 'sinful' actions of the squatters, Guardian William Thomas noted that he had 'never anticipated the trustees would hand over their reserve to squatters', but declined to judge on one of the four men. He assured himself that Aitkin 'is too honest and feeling a gentleman to be a party to so iniquitous a step'.[99] Thomas retained no such confidence in the character of the remaining trustees.

After the eviction of Taungurung people from Acheron, Hugh Glass wrote to the Central Board seeking a guarantee that they would relinquish their claim on the run. The secretary of the Central Board, Brough Smythe, responded with a perfunctory and no doubt annoying response: 'It is the intention of the Board to retain possession of all Aboriginal reserves throughout the colony'. Brough Smythe did, however, request that Trustee Snodgrass 'be good enough to report on the subject of this letter and advise the Board as to the proper steps to be taken' regarding Acheron and Mohican.[100] Dissatisfied with Brough Smythe's answer, Glass took the issue to a higher authority to complain of 'very serious loss and inconvenience'. He asked the commissioner of land and survey if the government:

> Intended to retain possession of that portion of my licenced run known as Niagaron which had been used as a temporary reserve for the blacks or whether they intended to return it to me having purchased Mr Jones' run as a permanent reserve for them.[101]

97 Report, Robert Hickson to William Thomas, 18 November 1860, Mohican/Acheron Station June–December 1860, NAA, B312, Folio 43.
98 'Reserve for Aborigines County of Anglesey', Mohican/Acheron Station January–June 1860, NAA, B312, Item 2.
99 William Thomas to Central Board, 8 October 1860, Mohican/Acheron Station June–December 1860, NAA, B312, Folio 33.
100 Mohican/Acheron Station June–December 1860, NAA, B312, Item 3, Folios 24–25, 27.
101 Hugh Glass to Honourable Commissioner of Lands and Survey, 20 September 1860, Mohican/Acheron Station June–December 1860, NAA, B312, Item 3, Folios 24, 27.

Responding to this exertion of influence at their next meeting, the Central Board concluded on 24 September 1860 that:

> As the proposed reserve has (although occupied by the blacks) been never approved by the Governor in Council, it would be desirable that the Central Board for the Protection of Aborigines should decide whether the proposed reserve is required now that the Mohican station has been purchased for the use of the Aborigines. If recommended by the Central Board the reserve can be again submitted for the approval of the Governor in Council.[102]

Once again, the board asked Snodgrass 'to be so good as to furnish a report on the question'.[103] Aware that the eviction of the Taungurung had already taken place, and that delay would assist the squatters' cause, Snodgrass replied on 4 October 1860 that such a report 'necessitates listing the stock which I cannot conveniently do at present'.[104] With Snodgrass silent on the matter, the Central Board determined to write to Trustee John Maxwell for advice and information 'touching the removal of the blacks to Jones' station'.[105] Maxwell, who had business links with Hugh Glass, argued that no negative impacts were observed following the removal of the Taungurung from Acheron to Mohican. Instead, he championed the proximity and suitability of the Mohican run for Aboriginal occupation:

> I have the honour to say that I do not believe that the removal of the blacks from the reserve on the Acheron to Jones' has had the slightest effect on any of the [residents] on the establishment. The distance between the two places does not exceed two miles and … the latter country is more open and extensive [and] better adapted for their camping ground.[106]

Maxwell was aware that the Taungurung had embarked upon a permanent farming venture at Acheron Aboriginal Station, but he perpetuated the belief that Aboriginal land use centred upon itinerant hunting and temporary camping. He also asserted that the small numbers of Taungurung at the new Mohican Station reflected the demands of seasonal work patterns:

102 Mohican/Acheron Station June–December 1860, NAA, B312, Item 3, Folio 28.
103 Mohican/Acheron Station June–December 1860, NAA, B312, Item 3, Folio 28.
104 Transcript of letter, Snodgrass to Central Board, Mohican/Acheron Station January–June 1860, NAA, B312, Item 3, Folio 31.
105 Minute, 11 December 1860, Board Meeting Minutes 1860–1862, NAA, B335/0, Box 1, Folio 13.
106 John Maxwell, 'Cathkin' Merton to Brough Smyth, 21 December 1860, Mohican/Acheron Station January–June 1860, NAA, B312, Item 3, Folio 52.

> At the beginning of the season a few left for the purpose of shearing and washing sheep at the neighbouring stations, the Chief was here with a few others, I heard of no complaint except a shortage of tea and sugar and all expressed their intention of returning in a short time.[107]

Trustee John Maxwell suggested that Aboriginal disquiet over Mohican Station was temporary and minor. Generational oral knowledge maintained by Taungurung people presents a very different interpretation of the same historic episode. Taungurung Elders were increasingly upset by the duplicity of the settlers and officials who forced them to move from Acheron to Mohican and then, as revealed in Chapter 3, briefly back to Acheron again. The Elders, as Uncle Roy recalls, refused to relocate voluntarily and were forcibly removed from Acheron, saying 'No! We take nothing but our own land'.[108] Taungurung perspectives on the importance, function and rightful possession of land were, and are, starkly divergent to the powerful vested interests of squatters and their representatives in government.

Conclusion: 'It would be well for the Aborigines to themselves select the localities'

Aboriginal people chose to settle on Acheron Station because it was a culturally meaningful site that also promised to fulfil their farming aspirations. Guardian William Thomas understood this and, recalling the failed protectorate experiment, advocated for an extension of the Aboriginal reserve system. He envisaged five Aboriginal settlements on 'the banks of the Murray, or upper branches of most the out of the way rivers':

> It would be well for the Aborigines to themselves select the localities … Hitherto white-man have selected the spots. White-man's taste is widely different to the Aboriginal; that was powerfully exemplified to me in my late accompanying the Upper Goulburn delegates to their 'Goshen' … no white-man, not even

---

107 John Maxwell, 'Cathkin' Merton to Brough Smyth, 21 December 1860, Mohican/Acheron Station January–June 1860, NAA, B312, Item 3, Folio 52.
108 Roy Patterson, in conversation with Jennifer Jones, 3 March 2016, DS3001137.

the most zealous missionary—would have selected such a spot. My impression is, that much of the ill-success attending previous exertions has been through this—drawing them to a locality in which they had no interest, or felt no pleasure in encamping on.[109]

Thomas's predominantly Christian readership understood the mobilisation of this well-known biblical story. 'Goshen' is the Hebrew name for a place in ancient Egypt, where the patriarch Joseph established a refuge for his family during drought and famine. Thomas linked the success of Aboriginal settlements to Godly intention and the selection of land by Aboriginal people themselves. This parallel also predicts impending banishment: as the Israelites fled from Egypt, so the Taungurung were evicted from their Goshen.

109 Printed copy of William Thomas's recommendations, 20 July 1860, Mohican/Acheron Station January–June 1860, NAA, B312, Item 3, Folio 5.

3

Mohican Aboriginal Station: 'Forced miles from the spot they cherished'

After the Taungurung clans had been evicted from Acheron Aboriginal Station, the majority refused to relocate to the new site at Mohican Station, despite instruction to do so by authorities. Forced to abandon their crops and infrastructure on their chosen reserve, Taungurung leaders made it known that they considered Mohican Station, just over 3 miles (5 km) to the south, to be unsuitable for agriculture and too cold for permanent occupation. Superintendent Robert Hickson reported the en masse departure of Taungurung people to his superiors in December 1860, noting that '48 blacks left in a body and are now scattered'.[1] Oral knowledge handed down to Uncle Roy Patterson suggests, to the contrary, that the clans had not scattered 'as heretofore among the neighbouring stations'.[2] Instead, they had regrouped at another culturally significant camping site. Uncle Roy narrates the impetus for this decision:

1   Robert Hickson, Report to Peter Snodgrass Esq, 5 December 1860, Mohican/Acheron Station January–June 1860, NAA, B312, Item 3, Folios 46A–49.
2   William Thomas, Report, 10 November 1860, Mohican/Acheron Station January–June 1860, NAA, B312, Item 3, Folio 41.

Just when the Aboriginal people thought, 'We have got a good place here' they pushed them off. They went down to Narbethong where the old hotel is. It's a good camp, plenty of water, plenty of food, flat land and the old man said, 'Sit down, we make camp', so the white people left them there on their own.[3]

Guardian William Thomas believed that further efforts to relocate the Aboriginal community would 'prove an utter failure', not due to 'any act of the Aborigines', but as the result of 'being forced miles from the spot they cherished and which I assured them Government would most sacredly retain for them'. Nevertheless, Thomas considered it to be 'much regretted that the Goulburn Blacks continue in their present state of mind'. According to Thomas, their stubborn resolve threatened the viability of the relocated reserve. Rather than focusing on the circumstances that prompted the Taungurung to boycott the move, officials fretted over 'all the expense laid upon the Acheron River reserve' and the likely loss of progress towards the stated goal of civilisation.[4]

The most significant outcome of the Taungurung refusal to relocate to the new station (referred to variously as 'Jones's station', 'Upper Acheron Station' and 'Mohican Station') by 'the majority of the young men and children' was that Superintendent Hickson was deprived of able-bodied workers. In January 1861, Hickson reported that these workers had 'not returned since the removal of the station' and made several urgent requests to employ a European labourer to assist him with the 'great deal of clearing and fencing to be done before any crops can be put in'. Extra assistance was also required because, in Hickson's view, 'the Blacks are so lazy and there is much to be done'.[5] Hickson's opinion of Aboriginal workers was common among Europeans at the time. Such views overlooked or misunderstood cultural differences that influenced Aboriginal attitudes to participation in the capitalist economy. Capitalism is future-oriented and based upon personal acquisition, while Aboriginal work, including labour-intensive ceremony, food gathering and the social exchange of goods, is shaped by spiritual meaning and obligations oriented towards clan welfare. Aboriginal labour is also governed by the need to sustain rather than exploit finite natural resources.[6] The enthusiastic investment

---

3   Roy Patterson, in conversation with Jennifer Jones, 3 March 2016, DS3001137.

4   William Thomas, Report, 8 October 1860, Mohican/Acheron Station June–December 1860, NAA, B312, Item 3, Folio 33-33A.

5   Robert Hickson to Robert Brough Smyth, 28 February 1861, Mohican Acheron Station January–June 1861, NAA, B312, Item 4, Folios 11–11A.

6   Broome, 'Aboriginal Workers', 207; Pascoe, *Dark Emu*.

of Aboriginal labour in the preparation of Acheron Station for long-term settlement, and obvious disappointment of Taungurung farmers when their crops were abandoned to hungry cattle, indicates that Aboriginal people entered the settler economy motivated by their own philosophy of work. Taungurung understanding of farming clearly focused less upon the production of a saleable harvest than it did upon the capacity to maintain community life on culturally significant land.

Robert Hickson's own peculiar contribution to the labour shortage at the new Mohican Aboriginal Station (explained below) also deserves consideration because it draws attention to complex multilateral relationships between local settlers, Aboriginal people and the officials employed to protect and improve them.[7] In early 1861, Trustee Peter Snodgrass had finally heeded Hickson's complaints and appointed a European worker to assist with the development of the new run. This worker resigned within the month, after Hickson accused him of 'neglect of duty', and 'denounce[d] the agricultural labourer as a spy'.[8] Hickson's sense of embattlement reflected the widening breach between himself and Trustee Peter Snodgrass, who had recruited the worker. Hickson's paranoia centred around Aboriginal independence and the influence of local squatters on daily operations at the settlement.

Hickson needed to harness free Aboriginal labour to develop required infrastructure without incurring expense beyond that of materials. Missionaries and protectors then believed that cash payments were inappropriate for Aboriginal people. As Christina Twomey has noted, rations were viewed as a more suitable form of recompense because of the low position of Aboriginal people on an 'imagined "scale" of civilisation'.[9] Hickson had to secure this free labour in competition with local squatters, who sought Aboriginal seasonal workers for waged roles that also promised a degree of autonomy. This offsite work also increased Aboriginal contact with the wider settler community. Hickson's attempts to control Aboriginal labour and manage tensions caused by cross-racial proximity undermined his relationships with local settlers, alienated the Aboriginal community and frustrated the trustees who held authority over him.

---

7   Twomey, 'Vagrancy, Indolence and Ignorance', 105.
8   Robert Hickson to Robert Brough Smyth, 28 February 1861, Mohican Acheron Station January–June 1861, NAA, B312, Item 4, Folios 11–11A; Peter Snodgrass to Robert Brough Smyth, 13 May 1861, Mohican Acheron Station January–June 1861, NAA, B312, Item 4, Folio 33.
9   Twomey, 'Vagrancy, Indolence and Ignorance', 103.

From 'the most comfortable house on the River Goulburn' to 'living under bark'

Robert Hickson was still struggling to establish infrastructure and order on the Aboriginal station after three months at the new location. Housing was an acute concern, as Hickson's family had been 'living under bark' or had been 'dependent upon casual accommodation [provided] by neighbouring settlers'.[10] Hickson's first child, Elizabeth Adelaide, was born at Acheron on 28 January 1860, and his second, Frances Mary, at Yea on 8 July 1861. In this colder country, Hickson was likely anxious to secure a basic hut for his toddler and pregnant wife 'prior to the commencement of the winter'. Works had been underway for such a hut at Acheron, but the commissioner of lands and survey had ordered 'the suspension of building operations' once squatter objections to the settlement came to notice.[11] Hickson reminded the Central Board Appointed to Watch Over the Interests of Aborigines of his need for building materials, arguing that in this colder location it would be 'impossible to pass the winter in our house without doors or floors'.[12] Hickson was an educated and respectable man drawn from an elevated social background, but his commitment to Christian duty led him to accept the meagre station accommodation. Both Hickson and his wife were apparently motivated by 'a passionate connection' to evangelical Anglicanism.[13]

Robert Hickson was granted the role as superintendent of Acheron Aboriginal Station on 15 April 1859, aged 22. He married 26-year-old Emily Villeneuve Watton just a few weeks later, on 4 May 1859, at Warrenbayne, a station held by Emily's brother-in-law, James Moore, near Violet Town.[14] Hickson and Emily came from gentle families that were well connected in Britain and within the colonies. Hickson's family has been described as 'Anglo-Irish elite' and Emily's as 'landed gentry'.[15] Although hailing from privileged origins, Emily had already experienced

---

10   Subjects comprised in papers handed to Mr Brough Smyth for the consideration of the Board for Protection of Aborigines, 5 June 1860, Board Meeting Minutes 1860–1862, NAA, B335/0, Box 1, Folios 44–43.

11   Minute, 5 June 1860, Board Meeting Minutes 1860–1862, NAA, B335/0, Box 1, Folios 44–43.

12   Robert Hickson to Robert Brough Smyth, 26 March 1861, Mohican Acheron Station January–June 1861, NAA, B312, Item 4, Folio 16.

13   Hickson was paid £183 in 1860 and £200 in 1861, Victoria, Parliament, *First Report of Central Board*, 35, 10; Hutchinson, 'The Worcester Circle'.

14   Registration Number 1251.

15   Hutchinson, 'The Worcester Circle'.

seven years living and working on an Aboriginal station. Her father, Dr John Edward Watton, replaced the 'hated protector' Charles Sievwright at Mount Rouse Aboriginal Station in the Western District and served as medical officer/assistant protector from 1842 to 1849.[16] William Thomas noted in his journal on 21 May 1859 that Emily Hickson had 'for years had Blacks under her charge teaching tiny children to needlework, wash and read at Mount Rouse Aboriginal Station being the daughter of the late Amiable Protector there Dr Wooton [sic]'.[17] John Watton, 'squatter and doctor', arrived in Victoria in 1839 and established his family in the Western District. As Paul de Serville noted, his family soon 'made good matches', with his elder daughters 'integrated with the squattocracy' in the Western District.[18] These connections explain why Watton was perceived to be 'more popular with the local squatters' than the vilified Sievwright.[19] The family moved to the Goulburn River Valley when son-in-law James Moore invested in Barjarg Station near Mansfield in 1849.[20] Another of John Watton's daughters, Mary Sophia, made a less elevated match when she wed John Mayne Conolly in 1857. Connolly, a station manager in the Western District, moved to Hugh Glass's Niagaroon Station in the Upper Goulburn in 1856, a position he then held for seven years.[21] Conolly thus had oversight of the run during the tumultuous period when his new brother-in-law, Robert Hickson, established Acheron Aboriginal Station within the boundaries of Niagaroon. This familial relationship advantaged both parties, as they were privy to insider information. For example, Mary Sophia Conolly, who was 'the lessee of part of the Niagaroon Station', petitioned for compensation after a fence was destroyed by fire on the property. She argued that she had information that 'the fire originated at the Reserve occupied by the Blacks' to support her claim.[22] The same channels alerted Hickson to the manoeuvres of local squatters as they attempted to undermine the Aboriginal station. Such knowledge perhaps explains why Hickson did not display the shocked surprise experienced

16 Victoria, Parliament, *First Report of Central Board*.

17 Journal entry, 21 May 1859, in Thomas, *Journal of William Thomas*, 212.

18 de Serville, *Port Phillip Gentlemen*, 205; *Port Phillip Patriot and Melbourne Advertiser*, 10 February 1842, 2.

19 *Mount Rouse Aboriginal Protectorate (Former)*, Victorian Heritage Database Report, 22 March 2004, accessed 13 June 2018, vhd.heritagecouncil.vic.gov.au/places/23746/download-report.

20 He later bought 'Benalla' on the Broken River and 'Warrenbayne' near Violet Town. Moore's close associates included Redmond Barry and Sir William Stawell, second chief justice of Victoria. Billis and Kenyon, *Pastoral Pioneers*.

21 Sutherland, *Victoria and its Metropolis*, 407.

22 Minute, 17 September 1860, Central Board Appointed to Watch Over the Interests of the Aborigines in the Colony of Victoria, NAA, B314, Item 1.

by Guardian William Thomas upon the forced relocation of the station.[23] Tensions caused by the controversial location of the Aboriginal station may also have affected the Conolly's tenure at Niagaroon. Conolly built a house between Niagaroon and Thornton stations prior to 1861, and was acknowledged as 'the first settler near Acheron township'.[24] Although well established and connected in the district, the family left the Upper Goulburn suddenly in 1862. The events that prompted this swift departure are discussed below. Conolly then selected land at Christmas Hills in the Upper Yarra region and called the property Niagaroon, perhaps indicating a degree of fond remembrance and regret over the relocation.[25]

Emily Hickson's brothers, John Ludlow Watton and William Henry Watton, also held property on the Upper Goulburn from 1854 to 1861 at Balham Hill (with various partners), 6 miles (9.6 km) east of Yea. The purchase of Balham Hill established the family in the best house of the district, a 'commodious' home built by Edward Cotton in 1843.[26] His brother John Cotton described Balham Hill as 'the most comfortable house on the River Goulburn'.[27] This 'brick dwelling house, woolshed, outhouses and stables' was Emily Watton's home for some three years until her mother's death in 1857.[28] She then lived 'with friends' at Warrenbayne until her marriage in 1859.[29] These Upper Goulburn connections explain how the couple came to be 'strongly recommended' by local dignitaries 'W. L. Ker Esqr JP, Aitkin Esqr JP and Snodgrass JP' when they applied for the positions of superintendent and matron of the Aboriginal station.[30] Robert and Emily Hickson were thus embedded in good society within

23 Thomas's letters of protest suggest that he was taken completely unawares. See, for example, William Thomas to Central Board, 22 November 1860, Mohican/Acheron Station June–December 1860, NAA, B312, Item 3, Folio 44.
24 The house is shown on Thomas Nixon's 1861 map of Niagaroon's pre-emptive section. Noble, *The Red Gate*, 26.
25 Noble, *The Red Gate*, 26; Sutherland, *Victoria and its Metropolis*; Ngaire von Sturmer to M. Rosalyn Shennan, 2 August 1983, Correspondence with Ngarie von Sturmer 1983–1986, State Library of Victoria (hereafter SLV), MS 12242, Box 2799/6.
26 John Cotton to William Cotton, 2 September 1843, Mackaness, *The Correspondence of John Cotton*, 26.
27 John Cotton to Marian Cotton December 1846, Mackaness, *The Correspondence of John Cotton*, 49.
28 'Squatting Run Files Balham Hill (No.171)', in Ngaire von Sturmer to M. Rosalyn Shennan, 29 December 1984, Correspondence with Ngarie von Sturmer 1983–1986, SLV, MS 12242, Box 2799/6.
29 Harriet Maria Ludlow Watton, Probate and Administration Files, PROV, VPRS 28/P1, Unit 4, Item 2/505.
30 Mohican/Acheron Station 1859, NAA, B312, Item 1, Folio 16.

the district when they accepted their posts, much as Dr John Watton had been integrated into Western District's squattocracy when he assumed his duties at Mount Rouse.

Religion, social status and mission outreach

Even in this early colonial period, when religion held a strong influence over life choices, Emily Hickson's move from the 'best house' in the Upper Goulburn district to living 'under bark' on Acheron Aboriginal Station might have provoked negative comment. A common prejudice fostered by early mission efforts to convert and civilise Aboriginal people, for example by Rev. Samuel Marsden, was the view that Aboriginal people were unresponsive to the gospel because, as 'degraded descendants of Ham', they were positioned so lowly on the chain of being.[31] This status made outreach by worker-missionaries drawn from the middle and lower classes most appropriate. The assistant protectors employed under the Port Phillip Protectorate system were characterised by this class positioning. The efforts of educated and cultured missionaries were thought more suitable among those perceived to be advanced on the cultural hierarchy, such as the Chinese or Maori.[32] Similar hierarchy-based arguments rationalised the muted success of the Church of England in colonial Australia. Upper Goulburn squatter John Cotton reflected in 1849, for example, that clergy of the Church of England 'do not go so much amongst the lower class of people as those of other sects. Is this from their having generally received a better education?' According to this reckoning, clergy without 'refinement of manners', including Roman Catholics and dissenters, were willing to send 'their emissaries throughout the country to procure the adherence of the great mass of people'.[33] Meanwhile, the Church of England hierarchy in Melbourne worried about the standard of available housing for clergy and refused to 'send a clergyman up here until a sufficient sum is raised to build a comfortable house for him'.[34] Hierarchical sensibilities were likely offended by Robert and Emily Hickson's acceptance of living

---

31 Harris, *One Blood*, 45.
32 See, for example, the arguments of Reverend Samuel Marsden in Yarwood, *Samuel Marsden*, 102, 112.
33 John Cotton to William Cotton, July 1849, in Mackaness, *The Correspondence of John Cotton*, 45.
34 Letter no. 53, John Cotton to William Cotton, July 1849, in Mackaness, *The Correspondence of John Cotton*, 45.

conditions little above that afforded Indigenous residents. Such personal sacrifice aligned with the emergent principles of evangelical 'faith mission' ideals, as expounded by Hudson Taylor's China Inland Mission in 1865.[35]

Religion in the Upper Goulburn in the period was closely linked to social status and responsibility. By 1857, when attempts by locals to attract a permanent minister from any Protestant tradition had failed, a group of 'prominent Protestant squatters' became sufficiently concerned for the 'religious training of their children' that they collaborated to engage a lay preacher in the Upper Goulburn.[36] The Muddy Creek Mission, an interdenominational evangelical outreach, offered the first permanent religious services in the Upper Goulburn in January 1857. The mission subscription list provides insight into both the religious feelings and the social hierarchy of squatters neighbouring the Aboriginal station. Religious subscription lists of the period, according to Rowan Strong, can be read as reflecting social position and degree of personal wealth, as well as interest in religious affairs.[37] It is, therefore, pertinent to note the contribution of locals who had an association with both the Aboriginal station and the religious mission. Hugh Glass, who orchestrated the swift removal of the Aboriginal station from Acheron to Mohican, made the largest annual subscription to the Muddy Creek Mission, at £67. Trustee of Acheron/ Mohican Aboriginal Station Donald Mackenzie pledged £35, and fellow Trustee John Christie Aitken pledged £25. The Watton brothers of Balham Hill also pledged £25, as did Henry Johnson, whose family association with the Aboriginal station was to cause significant reputational damage in 1861. John Mayne Conolly, manager of Niagaroon and a Watton brother-in-law, donated £15, and Stephen Jones, then owner of Mohican Station, gave £1.[38] Any contribution by Robert and Emily Hickson, who married one year prior to the closure of this mission outreach, is unrecorded. The couple were not, however, without income, as were many who adhered to faith mission principles. The Central Board's budget estimates for 1861 record that the 'teacher and matron' at Acheron Station were allocated £200 per annum. This suggests that Hickson's acceptance of rustic housing conditions on the station represented an ethical choice, rather than a financial necessity. The standard of housing among upper-class

---

35   Longworth, 'Upon Past Ebenezers', 176.
36   Blanks, *The Story of Yea,* 177.
37   See, for example, Strong, 'The Colonial Religion of the Anglican Clergy'.
38   Noble, *The Red Gate,* 57; Blanks, *The Story of Yea,* 177.

rural families was then improving. By 1844, 'some settlers' were 'erecting good and substantial houses, some of wood, some of brick, and some of stone'. Upper Goulburn squatter John Cotton made these observations by way of comparison, concluding with satisfaction, 'but mine is at present the largest on the river'.[39]

The Hicksons' choice to undertake self-denying practices for the sake of their mission might have fostered and/or disappointed other expectations in their set. The local men who recommended their appointment, for example, may have anticipated grateful deference from Hickson. It might also have been expected that Hickson would emulate the management strategies of his late father-in-law Dr Watton at Mount Rouse Aboriginal Station. According to Lindsey Arkley, Watton consistently prioritised settler needs and sought government protection for settlers, even though evidence suggested that it was Aboriginal people who needed protection from lethal settler aggression. Watton also restricted his attentions to those within the reserve and 'never concern[ed] himself much with the blacks elsewhere in the district'.[40] Robert Hickson's understanding of his duties on Mohican Aboriginal Station, by contrast, set him in direct conflict with squatter interests. The resulting clash was exacerbated by a sex scandal, discussed below, that shocked gendered and racialised propriety, threatening the longevity of Hickson's tenure and the viability of the Aboriginal station itself. I suggest that the crisis of September 1861 might also have contributed to the withdrawal of Emily Hickson's extended family from the district. Genealogists puzzled at the sudden corporate removal of the Wattons from the Upper Goulburn when they studied the extended family, noting that the Watton circle apparently 'all left the area around 1862–1864'.[41] Shennan and von Sturmer observed that the family held firm opinions regarding their elevated social standing. Although the squattocracy was quite mobile in the period, as land reform legislation influenced relocation decisions, social embarrassment may have played a part in the relocation of Watton family members. This is particularly the case, according to Shennan and von Sturmer, when the behaviour of

---

39   John Cotton to William Cotton, April 1844, in Mackaness, *The Correspondence of John Cotton*, 48.

40   Arkley, *The Hated Protector*, 456.

41   Ngaire von Sturmer to M. Rosalyn Shennan, 29 March 1984, Correspondence with Ngarie von Sturmer 1983–1986, SLV, MS 12242, Box 2799/6; Ngaire von Sturmer to M. Rosalyn Shennan, 30 August 1984, Correspondence with Ngarie von Sturmer 1983–1986, SLV, MS 12242, Box 2799/6.

a brother-in-law was 'not up to the standard of the rest of the Watton clan families'.[42] Robert Hickson's management of Mohican Aboriginal Station in 1861–62 may have provided an exemplar.

'Mr Hickson's disagreement with Mr Snodgrass': Masculine leadership and deference

Robert Hickson had several pressing aims for the development of Mohican Aboriginal Station in the autumn of 1861, in addition to securing more adequate housing for his pregnant wife and young child. He needed to clear and enclose enough land for cereal crops prior to the onset of winter. Containing cattle was particularly urgent, as poor or absent fencing made it difficult to keep the station herd out of the crops, or from joining wild mobs in the surrounding hills. Extensive fencing was not yet a profitable investment for squatters without secure tenure, so they 'had no incentive to fence'.[43] According to Cuthbert Fetherstonhaugh, 'the Wattons of Balham Hill were the first in the district to fence their run in stringy bark saplings laid end on end—what was called a "snake fence". This was in 1854'.[44] As neighbouring squatters did not necessarily invest in fencing, it was still imperative, six years later, to protect seasonal plantings on Mohican Aboriginal Station. These infrastructure efforts were tested by unexpected calls upon able-bodied Aboriginal workers. Hickson complained to William Thomas of:

> Strangers constantly coming to this station tempting away either as guides or bullock drivers the natives who are the most useful and the most constant [in] attendance here. I am now left with a few aged blacks and a few young children who are too young to instruct. There are only two men who are able to work they are too much distracted to do so in consequence of this, and William Riching [the European labourer] leaves in a few days.[45]

---

42   von Sturmer and Shennan are referring here to J. M. Conelly, who they speculate was a 'a drunkard ner-do-well' and extend pity to his wife 'poor Mary Sophia, with seven children and running a boarding house at Christmas Hills 1884–1891/2'. Ngaire von Sturmer to M. Rosalyn Shennan, 30 August 1984, Correspondence with Ngarie von Sturmer 1983–1986, SLV, MS 12242, Box 2799/6.

43   Pickard, 'The Transition from Shepherding', 155.

44   Fetherstonhaugh, *After Many Days*, 74.

45   Robert Hickson to Robert Brough Smyth, 26 March 1861, Mohican Acheron Station January–June 1861, NAA, B312, Item 4, Folio 16.

William Thomas sympathised with Hickson's plight, as he noted in his letter to the Central Board:

> I can readily feel the position Mr Hickson, all Aboriginal establishments labour more or less under the like annoyance—nor do I know how in the present state of the law with Aborigines it can be prevented.[46]

Hickson was also annoyed that he could not make any expenditure or decisions about the development of the station without permission from the local trustees, who in turn could not distribute funds 'unless previously sanctioned by the Board'.[47] Hickson chaffed under such restrictions, particularly when expenditure was necessary, in his view, to develop station self-sufficiency. Although Hickson was aware of the need to seek 'authority' before undertaking development decisions, in March 1861 he was 'obliged to hire a European labourer for a few weeks enclosing a paddock for the cattle which must be completed at once'; he could not wait for the reply of his superior.[48]

Hickson's class and education probably influenced his desire to exercise leadership and to assume financial autonomy.[49] His father, John Annesley Hickson, was a military man from County Kerry, Ireland, who led a company of 'pensioner' soldiers to New Zealand in his retirement. Arriving in 1848 to serve in The Royal New Zealand Fencible Corps, men like Hickson's father illustrated the 'usefulness of the settled soldier' by protecting early settlers from dispossessed Maori, whose acts of retaliation had 'crystallize[d] settler antagonism' towards philanthropic efforts to protect Indigenous peoples.[50] John Hickson apparently expanded this

---

46   William Thomas to Mr R. B. Smyth, Secretary Central Aboriginal Board, 9 April 1861, Mohican Acheron Station January–June 1861, NAA, B312, Item 4, Folios 19–20A.

47   Minute, 20 August 1860, Board Meeting Minutes 1860–1862, B335/0 Box 1, Folio 27.

48   Robert Hickson, Acheron Station, 26 March 1861, Mohican Acheron Station January–June 1861, NAA, B312, Item 4, Folio 16.

49   Hickson's younger brother, Charles Alfred St George Hickson, was 'educated chiefly by his father, but completed his education at the Auckland Wesley College', which was established in 1844 and is New Zealand's oldest registered school. Robert Hickson presumably received a similar education. 'Stamp, Land Transfer, Etc., Departments', *The Cyclopedia of New Zealand*, accessed 7 February 2019, nzetc.victoria.ac.nz/tm/scholarly/tei-Cyc01Cycl-t1-body-d3-d15-d14.html. Two of Hickson's brothers became men of note in New Zealand, Charles Alfred St George Hickson was commissioner of stamps, and Richard J.S. Hickson obtained senior rank in the Treasury Department. *The Auckland Star*, 20 June 1907, 5.

50   Lester and Dussart, 'Trajectories of Protection', 216. Enlistees in the Royal New Zealand Fencibles, including Lieutenant Hickson, were granted a cottage and 1 acre of land in return for seven years of service. Wards, *The Shadow of the Land*, 373, 375.

landholding sufficiently to provide his son Robert (who was 11 when the family migrated to New Zealand) with the 'experience of agriculture from his youth' that convinced Guardian William Thomas to appoint him as supervisor of Acheron Aboriginal Station.[51] It thus becomes apparent that both Superintendent Robert Hickson and Matron Emily Hickson had childhoods that intersected with, and were shaped by, redemptive Indigenous protection projects, as well as settler campaigns against them.

From January to June 1861, Robert Hickson chose to exercise leadership at the Aboriginal station by commissioning a blacksmith to undertake necessary work, by hiring a European labourer to complete station fencing and by purchasing seed wheat for winter cropping—all without the permission of his superiors. These actions soon came to the notice of Peter Snodgrass, as on two occasions Hickson authorised salary expenditure and ordered contingencies to the value of £8/60 by countersigning Snodgrass's name on his behalf and purportedly without his knowledge.[52] Snodgrass subsequently wrote to the board complaining about mismanagement of the station:

> It has become my duty to point out to your Board that the Acheron Aboriginal Station cannot with advantage to the natives or my credit be permitted to remain under the management of the present superintendent Mr Hickson that gentleman being so deficient of those qualities upon which such a position requir[es] strength of mind, forbearance and common sense.
>
> I now request that your Board will be pleased to place some person in charge whose personal character will be some guarantee of his fitness for the management of the Acheron Station. My official connection with Mr Hickson has been a source of annoyance to me from the first and it is due to the Board that I should inform them that under no circumstances can it longer continue.[53]

This strongly worded complaint gained a swift response form the board, who were aware that a dispute between two local men of high standing would damage the Aboriginal station. The chair of the Central Board, Brough Smyth, wrote privately to Snodgrass, noting that:

---

51 Wards, *The Shadow of the Land*; journal entry, 21 May 1859, in Thomas, *Journal of William Thomas*, 212.

52 Mohican Acheron Station June–December 1861, NAA, B312, Item 5, Folio 11; Mohican Acheron Station January–June 1861, NAA, B312, Item 4, Folios 9–10.

53 Peter Snodgrass to the Secretary, Central Aboriginal Board, 11 April 1861, Mohican Acheron Station January–June 1861, NAA, B312, Item 4, Folios 23–22.

> The observations on Mr Hicksons' character would have been of smaller consequence and might have been overlooked by the Board if they had been made by a person occupying a different position to yours—but coming from you they have a peculiar force and significance—and if you persist in the statement, and satisfy the Board that Mr Hickson is wanting … the Board, I feel assured, will dismiss Mr Hickson.[54]

Given the seriousness of the charges, Smyth felt that Hickson's dismissal would occasion 'result[s]' that Snodgrass would 'not desire'. He therefore begged Snodgrass 'to be so good as to reconsider the charge you have made'.[55] Not sharing this interpretation of the matter, Snodgrass pursued Hickson's dismissal, informing him on 18 April 1861 that his employment would be terminated. The board then asked Hickson to travel to Melbourne to 'exculpate himself from complaints and charges brought against him'.[56] As Hickson had missed the scheduled coach from Yea to Melbourne, he hastily purchased a horse, but his choice was poor, and the horse died on the return journey.[57] Hickson then asked the board to pay £35 for the dead horse. This might be the circumstance Snodgrass was alluding to when he wrote to the board on 13 May 1861 incensed that Hickson had not been relieved of his post: 'the same abuses of system and worth of public money without any corresponding benefit [are] still to be continued under Mr Hickson's mismanagement'.[58] Snodgrass then resigned his custodianship of the Aboriginal station, relinquishing 'the responsibility which I have felt was attached to my position', and disassociated himself from Hickson, announcing that his letter 'terminates my correspondence upon this subject'.[59] When Hickson fronted the Central Board, he argued that 'all sinister results' at the station could be attributed:

> To the removal of the aborigines from the site of their predilection to Jones' Station which was much higher and colder and which had only a small patch of good land near it.[60]

---

54   Copy of letter, Robert Brough Smyth to Peter Snodgrass, 3 May 1861, Mohican Acheron Station January–June 1861, NAA, B312, Item 4, Folios 25–25A.

55   Copy of letter, Robert Brough Smyth to Peter Snodgrass, 3 May 1861, Mohican Acheron Station January–June 1861, NAA, B312, Item 4, Folios 25–25A.

56   Minute, 15 April 1861, Board Meeting Minutes 1860–1862, NAA, B335/0, Box 1, Folio 4.

57   Robert Hickson, 21 May 1861, Mohican Acheron Station January–June 1861, NAA, B312, Item 4, Folio 35.

58   Peter Snodgrass to Robert Brough Smyth, 13 May 1861, Mohican Acheron Station January–June 1861, NAA, B312, Item 4, Folio 33.

59   Peter Snodgrass to Robert Brough Smyth, 13 May 1861, Mohican Acheron Station January–June 1861, NAA, B312, Item 4, Folio 33.

60   Minute, 3 May 1860, Board Meeting Minutes 1860–1862, NAA, B335/0, Box 1, Folio 2.

The Central Board concurred with Hickson's view, and he remained unchastened by the disagreement with Snodgrass. Hickson therefore continued in his efforts to gain financial authority over the station, unabashed.

Hickson had clashed with Snodgrass over requests for necessary stores, including seed wheat and fresh bullocks required to plant winter crops. Snodgrass explained that such requests would 'have to wait [until] the estimates had passed for the aborigines'.[61] However, Hickson pressed for the provision regardless, writing to William Thomas in May 1861 and arguing that there was 'no time to be wasted putting [the crop] into the ground'.[62] Unbeknown to Hickson, Guardian William Thomas had suffered a stroke and was unable to respond. Hickson proceeded to buy wheat from neighbouring squatter Henry Johnson, without the required authority.

Hickson's purchase was noted on 14 June 1861: 'R. Hickson has purchased wheat and employed a labourer for field work in anticipation of authority'. The Central Board responded by directing Hickson 'not to purchase anything without authority'.[63] Denied monies for wheat he had already purchased and sown, Hickson borrowed funds to repay the debt from John Mayne Conolly, his brother-in-law, describing him as 'a neighbouring settler'.[64] To minimise unauthorised outlay, Hickson was obliged to discharge the ploughman, but he noted that the wheat he had sown 'is above ground and promises to be a fine crop'. He also suggested that 'if it is intended that the workings of this station should be continued I would request authority to hire European labour as it cannot be conducted without'.[65] Hickson's quest for authority was in vain, as the board had already taken a decision regarding future management of the Aboriginal station.

---

61 Robert Hickson to William Thomas, 23 May 1861, Mohican Acheron Station January–June 1861, NAA, B312, Item 4, Folio 37.

62 Robert Hickson to William Thomas, 23 May 1861, Mohican Acheron Station January–June 1861, NAA, B312, Item 4, Folio 37.

63 Note, 14 June 1861, re Robert Hickson to William Thomas, 23 May 1861, Mohican Acheron Station January–June 1861, NAA, B312, Item 4, Folio 4.

64 Robert Hickson to Robert Brough Smyth, 23 December 1861, Mohican Acheron Station June–December 1861, NAA, B312, Item 5, Folios 48–48A.

65 Robert Hickson to Robert Brough Smyth, 18 July 1861, Mohican Acheron Station June–December 1861, NAA, B312, Item 5, Folio 3.

On 9 July 1861, the Central Board identified John Green as a suitable alternative manager. Green was a Scottish lay preacher working with Wurundjeri people on the Upper Yarra. He had been lobbying for an Aboriginal 'refuge and school' in the district since November 1860. The Central Board had been slow in their consideration of Green's proposal, twice postponing site visits and delaying a decision. They noted their 'reconsideration of a site for an aboriginal establishment at Upper Yarra' just days after complaints were raised against Robert Hickson at Acheron Aboriginal Station. John Green was offered the role of Inspector for Aborigines, which included some of the ailing William Thomas's duties.[66] Instead of establishing an Aboriginal station in the Upper Yarra, the board instructed Green to move to the Upper Goulburn and to assume oversight of Acheron/Mohican Aboriginal Station.

Records do not indicate when or how Robert Hickson heard of these decisions. Unfortunately for Hickson, a cross-racial sex scandal would further 'upset the settlers' and undermine his precarious tenure. On 2 September 1861, Hickson wrote to Brough Smyth informing him of a 'case having occurred on the Aboriginal Station under my charge'. The circumstance drew attention to the impossible demands of Hickson's position: making Aboriginal labour readily available to squatters, while simultaneously containing the same Aboriginal people on the station and preventing interactions between the races. Most feared was a cross-racial romantic liaison, such as that formed between Selina Johnson and Davy Hunter. The daughter of neighbouring squatter Henry Johnson, Selina 'about 19 years of age had gone missing from her home' and it was feared that she had 'gone off with the blacks'.[67]

'A white girl has gone off with the blacks and her father is anxious'

Selina Johnson disappeared from her home at Taggerty Station, which neighboured the Aboriginal reserve, just days after giving birth to an illegitimate child of mixed racial heritage. Her father Henry Johnson was a successful squatter who held Taggerty and Eglington stations. The son of a wealthy English mill owner who had trained as an engineer in Europe and

---

66   See Board Meeting Minutes 1860–1862, NAA, B335/0, Box 1, Folios 4, 6, 14.
67   Robert Hickson to Brough Smyth, 2 September 1861, Mohican Acheron Station June–December 1861, NAA, B312, Item 5, Folios 9–9A.

migrated to Australia against family wishes, Johnson married beneath his rank and produced an Upper Goulburn dynasty noted for their handsome looks and athletic bearing.[68] Johnson had objected to being 'surrounded by an Aboriginal reserve' when the location of Acheron Aboriginal Station was first surveyed. He complained in January 1860 that the location of the station was 'a hardship upon him, especially as an equally suitable place is available without interfering with anyone particularly'.[69] However, this fear of 'interference' did not prevent Johnson from employing Taungurung labourers on his station within the month. A 'mutual frequent connection' was thus established between young Selina Johnson and a certain 'young black man', Davy Hunter, who had been 'in Mr Johnson's employment for … eighteen months'. The couple had formed an understanding—'she consented to be his wife which he considers her to be'—but the relationship was not supported by Selina's family.[70] When Selina became pregnant, she 'would not acknowledge … the father of the child', but 'in due time the child … proved a black or half caste'.[71] Guardian Thomas reported that Selina and Davy had run away together after the birth of their baby, who they named James Wilson Boyd Johnson. Anxious to find the 'place of [Selina's] concealment', Henry Johnson contacted Robert Hickson and 'requested [him] to ask the blacks of her'. With the help of trackers, Robert Hickson discovered the couple and returned Selina to her parents. He noted that 'the child appeared to be a remarkably fine healthy boy'.[72] Despite this assessment, the baby died two weeks later, succumbing to an unspecified 'inflammation'.[73] The baby was buried by his grandfather, who eventually registered the birth and death eight weeks later in nearby Yea. Reports of the scandal had by then circulated beyond local confines to official circles, perhaps prompting Johnson to undertake the paperwork. Guardian William Thomas remarked that 'a highly respectable settler (who has been a judicial magistrate for many years)' had informed him of the affair. According to Thomas, 'this is the first instance of this kind in this or any of the neighbouring colonies' and:

---

68   Noble, *The Red Gate*.

69   F. Pinnifer, District Surveyor, to the Hon Commissioner of Lands and Survey, 12 January 1860, Mohican/Acheron Station January–June 1860, NAA, B312, Item 2, Folios 3–1A.

70   William Thomas to Robert Brough Smyth, 23 September 1861, Mohican Acheron Station June–December 1861, NAA, B312, Item 5, Folio 13; Robert Hickson to Robert Brough Smyth, 2 September 1861, Mohican Acheron Station June–December 1861, NAA, B312, Item 5, Folios 9–9A.

71   William Thomas to Robert Brough Smyth, 23 September 1861, Mohican Acheron Station June–December 1861, NAA, B312, Item 5, Folio 13.

72   Robert Hickson to Robert Brough Smyth, 2 September 1861, Mohican Acheron Station June–December 1861, NAA, B312, Item 5, Folios 9–9A.

73   Reed, 'White Girl', 12.

> Had the child lived I would have suggested (to prevent the disgraceful reoccurrence of the like) that the child should have been sworn to the black for maintenance, which as a matter of course he would not have been able to pay, and place him in prison for default.[74]

Henry Johnson also sought some form of punishment for Davy Hunter; despite the consensual nature of the relationship, he was reportedly 'very anxious that the case should be inquired into'.[75] However, Hunter was not apprehended or charged 'on the account of the girl concealing the circumstances for some months'.[76] The affair 'caused great sensation among the settlers in the Upper Goulburn' and drew further unwanted attention to Robert Hickson's management at the Aboriginal station.[77]

Embarrassed by this scandal and other failures at Mohican Station the Central Board was forced to make a public statement. Tabled in the Victorian parliament on 24 September 1861 and reproduced in *The Argus* on 15 October 1861, the *First Report of Central Board* argued that the change from Acheron to Mohican had not proven beneficial. The report was careful to exonerate the board and to blame unnamed vested interests:[78]

> Having no personal knowledge of the localities, and under the impression that the removal would be beneficial to the blacks, the Board on consideration of the evidence submitted to them, advised the Government to purchase Jones's Station (an arrangement all but completed when first brought under their notice).[79]

The report continued:

> Whether due to improper management, or to the unsuitableness of the site, or both combined, it is certain that the blacks have almost ceased to frequent the new reserve.[80]

---

74   William Thomas to Robert Brough Smyth, 23 September 1861, Mohican Acheron Station June–December 1861, NAA, B312, Item 5, Folio 13.

75   William Thomas to Robert Brough Smyth, 23 September 1861, Mohican Acheron Station June–December 1861, NAA, B312, Item 5, Folio 13.

76   Mohican Acheron Station June–December 1861, NAA, B312, Item 5, Folio 9A.

77   Mohican Acheron Station June–December 1861, NAA, B312, Item 5, Folio 14.

78   Victoria, Parliament, *The Victorian Hansard*, 23 September, 169; 'The Aborigines', *The Argus*, 15 October 1861, 7.

79   Victoria, Parliament, *First Report of Central Board*, 4.

80   Victoria, Parliament, *First Report of Central Board*, 4–5.

The board was also of the view that it was 'more especially' concerning that 'one of the Trustees, Mr. Snodgrass, M.L.A., had expressed himself as dissatisfied with the management of the station generally'. The gentlemen concluded that:

> The new station [Mohican] must be abandoned ... The management and general expenses of the establishment have consumed more of the funds placed at the disposal of the Board than the number of blacks frequenting the reserve would warrant, and arrangements are about to be made which, it is hoped, will improve the condition of the natives, and certainly very largely reduce the cost of their maintenance.[81]

This public statement represented a significant shift in sentiment, from a board determined to support Hickson and prepared to sacrifice Snodgrass, to a board supportive of Snodgrass and critical of Hickson. Although there is no direct evidence that the Johnson–Hunter scandal influenced this change of mind, the report emphasised that the board sought statements from 'the gentlemen in the neighbourhood' and some 'old settlers' to establish why there was such an 'extraordinary change' in the fortunes of the Aboriginal station.

The board sent Rev. John Green to assess the conditions on Mohican, instructing him to furnish a report. Green arrived at Mohican Station on 10 October 1861, just four weeks after baby James Johnson had died. His roll call of station residents noted with an asterisk that Davy, aged 22, was the 'father of the white woman's child' and that 'the woman wants to marry him'.[82] Green also reported that the settlement was in 'a very unsatisfactory condition', with numbers dwindling to only 16 people. He observed that gardens and cultivation paddocks that had been prepared by a meagre Taungurung workforce 'won't give good crops'.[83] Green also recorded Taungurung requests to move back to Acheron Station:

> The blacks opinion on the whole matter; they do not like Mr and Mrs Hickson they say that 'they are no good for black fellow and lubra Hickson too proud'. They say 'Governor very good to black fellow and black lubra give them plenty food and clothing'. They

---

81   Victoria, Parliament, *First Report of Central Board*, 5.
82   John Green, Acheron Aboriginal Station, 18 October 1861, Mohican Acheron Station June–December 1861, NAA, B312, Item 5, Folio 24.
83   John Green, Acheron Aboriginal Station, 18 October 1861, Mohican Acheron Station June–December 1861, NAA, B312, Item 5, Folio 26.

say that this station 'no good too cold plenty work no wheat no potatoes'. They say 'old station very good plenty wheat, potatoes and cabbages plenty everything'. They say the Governor give them the old station that by and by black fellow need no more things from him, black fellow by himself'. They want to get liberty to ride in wild unbranded cattle that are on this station.[84]

Green's transcription of Taungurung opinion provides mediated but nevertheless rare evidence of their assessment of Mohican Station and continuing ambition for self-determination. Taungurung leaders wanted to become self-supporting and to return to their chosen site at Acheron Station. They identified a viable revenue stream, the 'wild unbranded cattle' on the station, and asked for permission to 'ride [the cattle] in' so that 'by and by black fellow need no more things from [the Governor]'. Taungurung men were skilled station hands, working with cattle, sheep and horses prior to the introduction of fences in the Upper Goulburn. Men were 'employed to ride the boundaries' herding stock back onto the runs.[85] Drives were also intermittently conducted to round up horses and cattle 'gone wild' in the ranges.[86] For example, Cuthbert Fetherstonhaugh recalled the 'fine times' he had helping James Webster of Beaumonto near Yea to 'herd some wild cattle on the mountains', mustering them 'out of the scrubby river lands and out of the rough ranges at the head of the Muddy Creek'.[87] Fetherstonhaugh called to mind the exploits of an unnamed Taungurung man, described only as 'Webster's blackboy', who:

> Did a smart thing. He was also heading some cattle on the side of a steep range, and he had either to jump through the fork of a tree about three feet off the ground or pull back and let the cattle go. He never faltered, and the little horse jumped through the fork without grazing the darkie's legs, and the cattle were duly headed.[88]

This feat, c. 1855, suggests that skilled Taungurung workers could have successfully driven unbranded cattle from the hills surrounding Mohican Station in 1861 to secure a more autonomous future.

---

84   John Green, Acheron Aboriginal Station, 18 October 1861, Mohican Acheron Station June–December 1861, NAA, B312, Item 5, Folio 24.
85   Fetherstonhaugh, *After Many Days*, 74.
86   Fetherstonhaugh, *After Many Days*, 76.
87   Fetherstonhaugh, *After Many Days*, 76.
88   Fetherstonhaugh, *After Many Days*, 86–87.

Conclusion: A short career in Aboriginal protection

Robert Hickson's next actions undermined any confidence that the Central Board retained in him. On 30 October 1861, just weeks after Rev. Green's report had reminded the board of the troubles at Mohican, Hickson wrote an impertinent note attempting to curtail Indigenous movement and to retain able-bodied workers for the Aboriginal station. His note was addressed to Trustee John Christie Aitken, a 'considerable pastoralist' and gentlemen who held 'extensive chains of stations comprising all the country east of the Acheron and south of the Goulburn' between 1846 and 1866.[89] Hickson's letter accused Aitken of interfering with the affairs of the Aboriginal station, even though Aitken held a position as trustee. According to Hickson's account, Aitken already had Aboriginal shearers working on his property when he sought additional labourers to strip bark without authorisation. Therefore, Hickson wrote to Aitken:

> I did not understand that you required any blacks but the shearers but I believe your brother came over here on Sunday last by your orders and [requested] King Cotton and [several] lubras to strip bark for you and they left for your station last Thursday. I am sorry to say that I cannot possibly give [my permission] to go with these blacks as it is against the rules of this establishment and I would be obliged if you will send them back at once.[90]

Aitken was infuriated by Hickson's impertinence, replying immediately:

> I am in receipt of your extraordinary note. I have always understood that it is the wish of the Central Board that the Blacks should be employed and encouraged to take employment from the neighbouring settlers. It will be my duty to ascertain whether this is the cure or not vis I shall address the Board on the subject. I would only observe that I had relatively little to do with the blacks coming down—all with the exception of Old King and lubra. They intended for weeks past to come down to cut bark.[91]

---

89   de Serville, *Port Phillip Gentlemen*; Noble, *The Red Gate*, 13.
90   Robert Hickson to John C. Aitken Esq., 30 October 1861, Mohican Acheron Station June–December 1861, NAA B312, Item 5, Folio 29.
91   John Aitken [to Robert Hickson], 30 October 1861, Mohican Acheron Station June–December 1861, NAA, B312, Item 5, Folios 28–28A.

After noting Taungurung agency and intention, Aitken returned to the impudence of Hickson's intervention in his affairs: 'It seems to me you are out of you[r] [station] writing such a letter and taking upon yourself such a position'.[92] Aitken was clearly annoyed by Hickson's attempts to curtail autonomous Aboriginal movement, particularly where they impinged upon long established and mutually beneficial understandings about employment on neighbouring stations.

John Green's assessment of Mohican Station, dated 18 October 1861, was penned two weeks before Hickson's clash with John Aitken. This report found Mohican in 'a very unsatisfactory condition', as Hickson had alienated the 'gentlemen in the neighbourhood' and the Taungurung were 'impertinent' in response to his exertions of authority.[93] Two months after Green lodged his report, and just over two weeks after his clash with Aitken, Robert Hickson was forced to address persistent local gossip about his alleged deceitful conduct and abuse of financial authority. Hickson wrote to Brough Smyth on 19 November 1861, recounting that:

> I have just been told by Mr Ker of Killingsworth near Yea that Mr Snodgrass had informed him that you had shown him an account which I had sent to you for payment in which I had signed. I remember in billing up the account I wrote Mr Snodgrass as my authority for having the work done but I was under the impression that I enquired to do so. It is [quite] impossible that there was any intention to forge Mr Snodgrass' name as I had his authority to have the work performed.[94]

Hickson clearly retained some influential local allies. His informant, William Leyden Ker, a respected gentleman, had been appointed a special territorial magistrate in 1850 and was a member of the first Victorian Roads Board in 1869. A Scottish Episcopalian by background, Ker was known in the Yea district as a 'strong churchman'.[95] A shared understanding of religious values perhaps supported Hickson's claims to innocence. Records clearly show that Hickson had indeed signed Snodgrass's name on station accounts; Hickson's characteristically severe cursive is

---

92   John Aitken [to Robert Hickson], 30 October 1861, Mohican Acheron Station June–December 1861, NAA, B312, Item 5, Folios 28–28A.

93   John Green, Acheron Aboriginal Station, 18 October 1861, Mohican Acheron Station June–December 1861, NAA, B312, Item 5, Folio 26.

94   Robert Hickson to Brough Smyth, 19 November 1861, Mohican Acheron Station June–December 1861, NAA, B312, Item 5, Folios 40–40A.

95   Blanks, *The Story of Yea*, 86.

completely undisguised. Hickson signed Snodgrass's name on an account that reached the Central Board on 18 July 1861. He had previously signed accounts totalling £8/60 in the same manner; these reached Treasury on 26 June 1861.[96] Hickson continued to use Snodgrass's authority to make purchases for several months after Snodgrass had resigned as a trustee. Hickson noted in a letter to Brough Smyth on 6 September 1861 that he had not communicated with Snodgrass since 21 April 1861; yet, he continued to send Snodgrass his monthly report and showed surprise that Snodgrass had not 'acknowledged the receipt of my returns'.[97] Hickson seemed unaware of Snodgrass's resignation nearly four months after the event. This draws attention to Hickson's isolation within his own very small social circle in the Upper Goulburn, even before the birth and death of baby James Johnson prompted his complete fall from grace.

Hickson was informed on 4 January 1862 that it was the opinion of the Central Board that he was 'unfitted to be the manager of an Aboriginal station'. It was suggested that he should resign his office at the end of three months, but Hickson sought more immediate separation.[98] He removed his family from the settlement on 9 February 1862, noting that he could no longer 'expose them … to the impertinence of the Aborigines who will not obey me in anything since they were informed that I had no authority over them'.[99] On 11 March 1862, Rev. John Green was directed by the board to 'take steps to break up [Mohican] station by dismissing the servants and disposing of the stock'.[100]

---

96   Single salary account £5 William Richings, Mohican Acheron Station January–June 1861, NAA, B312, Item 4, Folio 9; memo for L. Morton, N.D., Mohican Acheron Station June–December 1861, NAA, B312, Item 5, Folios 11–11A.
97   Robert Hickson to Robert Brough Smyth, 6 September 1861, Mohican Acheron Station June–December 1861, NAA, B312, Item 5, Folio 12.
98   Robert Hickson to Robert Brough Smyth, 23 January 1862, Acheron Station 1862, NAA, B312, Item 6, Folio 3.
99   Robert Hickson to Brough Smyth, 13 February 1862, Acheron Station 1862, NAA, B312, Item 6, Folio 9.
100 Minute, 11 March 1862, Board Meeting Minutes 1860–1862, NAA, B335/0, Box 1, Folio 76.

4

Breaking up Mohican Aboriginal Station: 'They got sick of being shunted around'

When the Central Board Appointed to Watch Over the Interests of Aborigines announced in its annual report in 1861 that Mohican Aboriginal Station would be abandoned, they also foreshadowed, but did not detail, new arrangements that would 'improve the condition of the natives' and 'reduce the cost of their maintenance'.[1] It was the responsibility of the new manager, John Green, to find a more amenable location and to achieve the board's ambitious goals: to deliver more and cost less. Taungurung leaders had not consented to the previous removal from their favoured lands at Acheron, but they agreed with this relocation, despite the annoyance of leaving infrastructure and crops. Generational knowledge handed down to Uncle Roy Patterson suggests that:

> Soon Aboriginal people were growing food [at Mohican] up on the hill and there was timber that was good for building with [but] the white people shunted them from up there back down near to Cathedral Lane.[2]

---

1   Victoria, Parliament, *First Report of Central Board.*
2   Roy Patterson, in conversation with Jennifer Jones, 15 April 2016, DS3001141.

The historical record also notes that Taungurung leaders urged officials to return the settlement to the more productive Acheron site: 'Governor give them the old station and … black fellow need no more things from him'.[3] Taungurung leaders wanted to maintain community independence as much as possible. As noted in the previous chapter, many had refused to relocate to Mohican, camping at Narbethong instead, or favouring work and residence on neighbouring stations.

Squatter attitudes towards Aboriginal protection efforts in the district had proven both vexatious and contradictory. Squatters wished to maintain access to a ready workforce, but settler society was scandalised by cross-racial relationships enabled by proximity. These attitudes contextualised John Green's new round of negotiations with pastoralists Glass and Nash as he sought a more favourable location for the agricultural activities of the Aboriginal station. Glass and Nash had demonstrated their determination to maintain sole possession of Niagaroon in 1860. Green nevertheless approached the squatters optimistically, 'touching on the portion of land I wanted for the Aborigines'. This plot was adjoining 'the present Aboriginal Station' but within the confines of the run owned by Glass and Nash. Green was pleased (and perhaps surprised) to report that the pastoralists 'have no objections in giving the portion I pointed out to them viz about 200 acres'.[4] Although satisfied with this outcome, Green continued his search for suitable agricultural land. His criteria for an ideal site also included a degree of isolation from white society. Green noted in his letter to Brough Smyth that:

> I have found a better portion for farming on the present station about five miles north of the present farm. I therefore think that it would be better not to seek the portion off Glass and Nash's run as the Blacks are more willing to go to this part and they would be better out of the way of everyone.[5]

This new site within Mohican Station appeared to satisfy the requirements of all stakeholders; Taungurung farmers were 'more willing to go to this part' of Mohican Station because it brought them closer to their favoured lands at Acheron; Glass and Nash were not required to relinquish

---

3   John Green, Acheron Aboriginal Station, 18 October 1861, Mohican Acheron Station June–December 1861, NAA, B312, Item 5, Folio 24.
4   John Green, Acheron Station, to Robert Brough Smyth, 11 January 1862, Acheron Station 1862, NAA, B312, Item 6, Folio 1.
5   John Green, Acheron Station to Robert Brough Smyth, 11 January 1862, Acheron Station 1862, NAA, B312, Item 6, Folio 1.

200 acres; and, from a Central Board perspective, activities on the plot would decrease cross-racial interactions because it was sufficiently 'out of the way'. Secretary of the Central Board Brough Smyth supported the relocation, indicating his approval by a note in the margins of John Green's report, which read: 'Mr Green would want about £180 to put the new station in order. Should I ask for an advance?'[6] Oral history handed down to Uncle Roy also narrates this additional relocation, but takes a different focus. Generational knowledge of the move represents it as yet another instance of Aboriginal adaptation to settler imperatives:

> The white people shunted them from up there back down near to Cathedral Lane. They had only been there about a month, and just when the Aboriginal people thought, 'we have got a good place here' they took them down to Narbethong where the old hotel is.[7]

Government records do not detail the duration of Aboriginal settlement on this third farm site before the board's March 1862 decision to 'break up [Mohican] station' altogether.[8] Oral history suggests, however, that the Taungurung clans were very tired and disheartened by the board's vacillation. As Uncle Roy recounts:

> They weren't even asked; they were just told to get out. That's where the Wurundjeri mob come up and grabbed them and took them back to Coranderrk.[9]

The closure of Mohican Station would see the Taungurung clans forced to relinquish their lands and suffer removal to the territories of other groups in the Kulin Nation. The personal investments and priorities of John Green, as I will demonstrate below, had considerable influence on this outcome.

John Green (b. 1830) and his wife Mary (b. 1835) migrated to Australia from Scotland in 1857, and had been living and ministering in the Lilydale and Upper Yarra district for 18 months when Green was appointed an inspector of Aborigines by the Central Board on 9 July 1861.[10] Diane Barwick suggested that the life experiences and outlook

---

6   Acheron Station 1862, NAA, B312, Item 6, Folio 1.

7   Roy Patterson, in conversation with Jennifer Jones, 3 March 2016, DS3001137.

8   Minute, 11 March 1862, Board Meeting Minutes 1860–1862, B335/0, Box 1, Folio 76.

9   Roy Patterson, in conversation with Jennifer Jones, 12 July 2016, DS300154–56.

10   Minute, 9 July 1862, Central Board Appointed to Watch Over the Interests of the Aborigines in the Colony of Victoria, NAA, B314, Item 1.

of the Presbyterian couple fostered their warm connection with the young Wurundjeri families camped at Yering in the Upper Yarra Valley. According to Barwick:

> During 1860 [Green] rode over regularly to hold services for the young Wurundjeri couples camped at Yering, who were much the same age as himself and his wife. His wife accompanied him and their babies played together. The Scottish couple shared the puritanical views of their church but they had some sensitivity to the cultural and linguistic differences of minority groups … [Green's] income was little more than that the Wurundjeri men earned as farm labourers.[11]

Prior to his engagement as an inspector, Green derived financial support from the donations of a small local community of evangelical Presbyterians. He was thus working under 'faith mission' principles that nurtured a degree of fellow feeling between his family and the Wurundjeri at Yering. His strengthening commitment to the Wurundjeri can be gauged by his uptake of their campaign for a reserve of their own selection. Wurundjeri leader Wonga, explained his scheme to form a refuge and school in the Upper Yarra to William Thomas in October 1861. Wonga rejected lands selected by Thomas and the Central Board, and compared this request for land of his own choosing to the successful claim of the Taungurung clans:

> Wonga, having seen his friends the Goulburn Tribe comfortably provided for … said that he had looked out for a spot for the few blacks left in his tribe … he said, 'Marminarta you very good but black fellow no tell you look out that one country—I want like you get'em Goulburn blacks where black fellows likes'.[12]

John Green apparently accompanied Wonga to this meeting, and thereafter provided faithful support and advocacy for the scheme to procure culturally significant land chosen by Wurundjeri people themselves. Indeed, when William Thomas reflected on the meeting, he observed that 'Revd Mr Green of the Upper Yarra … had taken much interest in the Aborigines'.[13] Green and Thomas assisted Wonga to pursue the scheme, which was delayed and then postponed by the board in November 1860. Board officials still visited land selected by the deputy surveyor-general

---

11   Barwick, *Rebellion at Coranderrk*, 55.
12   William Thomas to Redmond Barry, 21 October 1861, quoted in Barwick, *Rebellion at Coranderrk*, 51.
13   Barwick, *Rebellion at Coranderrk*, 51.

in December 1860; however, they did not inspect the site identified by Wurundjeri leaders. Green and Wonga travelled from the Upper Yarra in January 1861 with a deputation protesting this failure.[14] The Wurundjeri request 'for an aboriginal establishment at Upper Yarra' was again tabled at the meeting of the Central Board on 15 April 1861.[15] On these occasions, Green demonstrated his capacity for dogged advocacy on behalf of the Wurundjeri clans.

Green's new role as manager of Mohican Station in the Upper Goulburn entailed official obligations towards other clans in the Kulin confederacy, not just the Wurundjeri. Green struggled to balance these dual and perhaps competing commitments. He was openly critical of Mohican Station and pessimistic regarding its prospects. His damning initial assessment, expressed in October 1861 just after the Johnson–Hunter scandal broke, was confirmed in February 1862 and then reiterated when he arrived to take charge of the station on 13 March 1862.

John Green was aware of the ongoing local impact of the relationship between Selina Johnson and Davy Hunter before he took up residence at Mohican Station. Davy Hunter had accompanied John Green on a trip to Melbourne in February 1862, attending an exhibition at the Museum of Illustration with Green and William Thomas. Thomas recorded Green's opinion of the love affair and its local impact in Upper Goulburn society. Thomas clearly had these circumstances in mind when he took close note of Davy Hunter's response to an illustration of Sleeping Beauty, seen at the museum. Thomas noted with apparent amusement that 'Davy is much struck with Sleeping Beauty, he says ["]Marnamuk White Lubra["] (this is the Scamp that got Mr Johnsons Daughter with child)'.[16] Amateur linguists of the period translated 'marnamuk' as meaning 'that one very good', indicating that the sleeping white woman was visually pleasing.[17] Thomas offered a sexualised reading of Davy Hunter's encounter with Sleeping Beauty, yet his observation was nevertheless infantalising,

---

14   Journal entry, 2 January 1861, in Thomas, *Journal of William Thomas*, 329.
15   Minute, 11 December 1860, Board Meeting Minutes 1860–1862, NAA, B335/0, Box 1, Folio 13; papers submitted for consideration, Central Board for Aborigines, 15 April 1861, Board Meeting Minutes 1860–1862, NAA, B335/0, Box 1, Folio 4.
16   Journal entry, 19 February 1862, in Thomas, *Journal of William Thomas*, 374.
17   The word '*marnamuk*' can be translated as meaning 'that one very good', according to Smyth, *The Aborigines of Victoria*, 129.

as a 'scamp' connotes a mischievous but likeable child. William Thomas was notably less benevolent in his recount of Selina Johnson's circumstances. Reflecting upon her commitment to Hunter, Thomas opined:

> Strange to say the taste, the Girl persists (by Green's statements) in marrying him when she is 21 Yrs of Age, the father to thwart this has offered even his Station to any white Man that will marry her (from Mr Green).[18]

Given that it was another two years before Henry Johnson managed to find a white man to marry Selina, it can be inferred that Johnson's 'offer' continued to circulate in Upper Goulburn society long after this February 1862 narration.[19] I suggest that Green's understanding of 'the state' of Mohican Station, recounted below, takes settler attitudes to Taungurung people into account:

> Sir I came here on the 13th and have taken everything off Mr Hickson here everything is in very bad order I will bring an account of all to Melbourne next week and I have not had time to write my mind about the state of things here being too busy putting the house in order for my family. PS I hope you will be able to come up with me next week and see the state.[20]

It is probable that John Green's assessment that 'everything is in very bad order' on Mohican Station included the social context, not just the condition of the station plant. Green wrote these words to Brough Smyth five days after making the hard trek up the Black's Spur. He explained that improving the unacceptably low standard of accommodation for his young family had delayed his writing. Here lies another difference between John Green and former manager Robert Hickson. Although they held similar faith-based commitments to their roles in Aboriginal protection, Green was apparently unwilling to accept the same raw living conditions that had satisfied Hickson. 'Faith mission' principles emergent in this era held that mission workers would 'live with adversity, hard work, and loneliness [and] accept sacrifice and suffering'.[21] This meant that an evangelistic agenda took precedence over other duties, which, in the

---

18   Journal entry, 19 February 1862, in Thomas, *Journal of William Thomas*, 374.
19   William Fenton, a 'general labourer', married Selina Johnson on 21 June 1864. Reed, 'White Girl', 18.
20   John Green to Robert Brough Smyth, 18 March 1862, Acheron Station 1862, NAA, B312, Item 6, Folio 11.
21   Longworth, 'Upon Past Ebenezers', 178.

context of Mohican Station, included practical activities oriented towards Aboriginal improvement. Yet Green was so busy 'putting the house in order for my family' that he had not found time to engage with his other duties, including drafting a more detailed complaint about conditions. Green clearly '[identified] with the culture' of the people he served, as endorsed by faith mission principles.[22] However, his identification seemed to centre on the interests and perspectives of Wurundjeri people.

John Green's responsibilities as an inspector entailed travel to Aboriginal stations around Victoria. Each return to Mohican Station provided fresh opportunity to reassess the liabilities of its location and amenities. Green communicated these disappointments at length in his report of 5 May 1862. It is worth reproducing these grievances in detail, as they provide insight into Green's view of Mohican Aboriginal Station. His report encompasses declining Aboriginal numbers, uncomfortable houses, failed crops, dying stock and wasted money. These woeful circumstances culminate with Green's suggestion that the settlement relocate to the Upper Yarra:

> I have the honour to inform you that I have returned to my headquarters (Acheron). I found on my return that a good many of the Blacks have left a few days after I left for Gippsland. Those who have left do not like this place. My Yarra Blacks do not like it either but while I remain here they will also remain. The number of blacks on the station at present are forty-three. Very little work has been done either by me or the blacks when at home have been busy repairing the houses which are in [a] very uncomfortable state. The blacks have been thrashing the wheat, there will only be about twenty bushels of it from fourteen bushels of seed.
>
> One cow and two bullocks have died since I came and the other two bullocks are scarcely able to walk. I believe that it is the cold that is killing the cattle there being plenty of grass. I will be obliged to send my horses to some other place as this is too cold for they are getting poorer everyday without any work. The horses left here when I went to Gippsland are a great deal poorer than those I rode. I can do but little agricultural work until I get more bullocks and a deal of blacksmith work for all the farming implements are out of order.

22   Longworth, 'Upon Past Ebenezers', 177.

> My candid opinion is that it would be folly for the Board to spend
> one sixpence more on this station as I do not think that it will pay
> the sixpences. But you should come up and see it yourself which
> would be more satisfactory to you and the Board. And I may state,
> should the Board give the blacks the portion of land on the Yarra
> then I believe that the greater part of the Goulburn blacks would
> settle down with the Yarra blacks as the Yarra blacks have done
> with them.[23]

According to John Green, a 'portion of land on the Yarra' would alleviate
the unhappy circumstances narrated so comprehensively in his letter.
Yet, this was not the key point gleaned by readers at the Central Board.
They focused instead upon the financial implications of the report, noting
'John Green … suggests that no more money should be expended by the
Board upon the station as he does not consider it will pay expenses'.[24] It is
unclear if Green was privy to the board's preferred reading of his report,
but he soon amended his approach to maximise benefit from the board's
preoccupation with financial performance.

Green's next report, submitted 6 June 1862, emphasised his decision to
give Mohican Station a 'fair trial'. This pronouncement, he noted, would
require sustained financial output by the board:

> The average number of blacks on the station the past month have
> been forty. Some of the young men work well and I believe will
> settle and do well if care is taken of them … It is a great pity that
> we have not a better Station but I will give it a fair trial, we will
> see after this year what it is like. If the Board has any money to
> spare I would ask for £30 to buy some bullocks for I cannot do
> anything without them, another of them has died since my last
> letter. I would also ask for authority to get some blacksmith work
> done. There have been three deaths since I came here; two of the
> Yarra tribe and one of the Goulburn, two adults and one child.[25]

Green clearly understood that the board did not 'have any money to spare'
when he made this request. William Thomas had recently experienced
repeated difficulty gaining promised funds for Mohican Station, including
on 9 May 1862, when he had noted in his journal that 'Mr Green's money

---

23   John Green to Robert Brough Smyth, 5 May 1862, Acheron Station 1862, NAA, B312, Item 6,
Folio 24.
24   Acheron Station 1862, NAA, B312, Item 6, Folio 25.
25   John Green to Robert Brough Smyth, 6 June 1862, Acheron Station 1862, NAA, B312, Item 6,
Folios 26–26A.

[was] not in the Treasury' as anticipated. After securing £36 of the promised amount, Thomas noted on 15 May that he again tried 'to get Green's money fail'.[26] By focusing upon expenditure and wasted resources at Mohican Station, Green drew attention to the perceived financial precarity of the board's activities. Parliament's chronic underfunding of the Central Board was to become a constant theme of future board reports. For example, their second report, published in 1862, noted that difficulty in arranging supplies for Aboriginal stations and depots 'has been occasioned mainly by the uncertainty of the provision to be made for the blacks by the Parliament'.[27] John Green finally engaged the attention of the Central Board by claiming that 'a better Station' would not drain the public purse in the same manner as Mohican. This more promising site was on the Upper Yarra, not the Upper Goulburn. The board finally concurred on 21 July 1862, announcing that 'Mr Green [is] to select the new site'.[28] The Central Board's second report noted that breaking up Acheron/Mohican Station would enable a more informal 'scheme of relief' to be implemented in the Upper Goulburn, one that would be 'free from the costs and embarrassments of a paid protectorate'.[29] From a government perspective, Mohican had indeed been costly and embarrassing.

'Come join us on our land, at Coranderrk'

When a piece of land was duly selected in the Upper Yarra Valley 'between Badger's Creek and the Watts River', much delay and uncertainty again beset the project. Objections that had forced the closure of Acheron and Mohican stations were again made—namely, that 'the site interfered injuriously with the rights of a neighbouring settler'.[30] The board now feared that 'neighbours' hostility would become a chronic hindrance' to any Aboriginal improvement activities and sought to delay another decision that would be unpopular with settlers.[31] John Green, however, had already complied with the board's directive to 'remove his station to the Watts River without delay' and his company had departed

26 Journal entry, 9 May and 15 May 1862, in Thomas, *Journal of William Thomas*, 380–81.
27 Victoria, Parliament, *Second Report of the Central Board*, 3.
28 Papers submitted for consideration, Central Board for Aborigines, 21 July 1862, Board Meeting Minutes 1860–1862, NAA, B335/0, Box 1, Folio 84.
29 Victoria, Parliament, *Second Report of the Central Board*, 5.
30 Victoria, Parliament, *Third Report of the Central Board*, 5–6.
31 Barwick, *Rebellion at Coranderrk*, 65.

Mohican Station for Coranderrk.[32] According to Diane Barwick, the board heard of local objections when 'the Greens and their four children (including a new baby), the Wurundjeri families and the younger Taungurung—40 in all—were already walking to the new reserve'.[33] The trekkers arrived in the Upper Yarra in March 1863 and selected a plot adjacent to the contested site. However, uncertainty of tenure continued to disrupt settlement plans until an opportunity arose for a deputation of Wurundjeri, Taungurung and Boonwurrung people to present their case at a public celebration held in honour of the Queen's birthday. On 26 May 1863, Aboriginal representatives presented 'a decorated address that expressed their affection for Queen Victoria' and indicated their right to both 'justice and recognition'.[34] Not long after, on 30 June 1863, the board achieved the hasty gazettal of Coranderrk, an outcome long attributed to the Kulin's strategic address to the sovereign.[35] The board justified the gazettal by arguing that the new station was 'well suited to the wants of the blacks, and in such a situation as to give satisfaction to all persons in the neighbourhood'.[36] Yet, Coranderrk Aboriginal Station was not 'well suited to the wants' of the Taungurung clans.

Generational knowledge handed down to Uncle Roy asserts that Taungurung Elders eventually consented to their peoples' removal to Coranderrk after they had been forced off the new Mohican camp and 'shunted away from Narbethong':

> Then Barak said to the people who had a bit of Wurundjeri, 'come join us on our land, at Coranderrk', but the Elders said 'no, we take nothing but our own land'. But when they were shunted away from Narbethong [again] they said, 'we will go down to Coranderrk, we don't want you to move us no more. We will go down to Coranderrk, down to Wurundjeri people on the mission'.[37]

Taungurung oral history emphasises the cumulative impact of broken promises and frequent relocation. By contrast, John Green's account of these negotiations highlighted the young Taungurung men's desire to gain improvement. On 28 July 1863, he observed:

---

32   Journal entry, 26 January 1863, in Thomas, *Journal of William Thomas*, 405.
33   Barwick, *Rebellion at Coranderrk*, 65–66.
34   Nugent, 'Politics of Memory', 104, 107.
35   See van Toorn, *Writing Never Arrives Naked*.
36   Victoria, Parliament, *Third Report of the Central Board*, 6.
37   Roy Patterson, in conversation with Jennifer Jones, 3 March 2016, DS3001137.

> So strong was the desire for improvement by this time among the young men belonging to the Goulburn, that they all at once consented to leave, and go to the Yarra. After the young men consented, the old ones consented also. And in the month of Feb'y when I started to proceed to the Yarra all the young men and two old ones started with me, and the others sent their children as a token that they would soon follow.[38]

From the perspective provided by Taungurung generational knowledge, this decision was not marked by a perceived division between young and old; rather, it represented a proud assertion of independence by Taungurung leaders:

> So, they walked down on their own without help from Wurundjeri or anybody else. They got sick of being shunted around so they walked down over the Cathedral, down over the Black Spur, and got into Coranderrk. They weren't shifted away from there until they went to Lake Tyers, but my ancestors didn't go; they stayed in Healesville.[39]

Uncle Roy narrates his family history and generational knowledge from a place-based perspective; his object is to demonstrate how Taungurung cultural inheritance was affected by forced removal and by a tenacious effort to maintain connection to Country:

> When Daunarung went to Coranderrk, they thought they had done the last shift, it was supposed to be the last shift; but every camp that they went to was supposed to be the last shift! I've done my last shift; I won't be moving off my ancestral Country.[40]

The Black Spur, now the bituminised main road from Narbethong to Healesville, can thus be understood as a 'storied landscape' that carried a disappointed but proud and independent people as they walked into exile at Coranderrk. These Taungurung Elders passed their knowledge and connection to traditional lands down to subsequent generations at Coranderrk, on the border of Taungurung Country.

---

38 Quoted in Barwick, *Rebellion at Coranderrk*, 67.
39 Roy Patterson, in conversation with Jennifer Jones, 3 March 2016, DS3001137.
40 Roy Patterson, in conversation with Jennifer Jones, 3 March 2016, DS3001137.

'To provide instruction for the children': The changing priorities of the Central Board

The removal of Taungurung clans to Wurundjeri Country coincided with another significant change made by the Central Board—a change of focus in Aboriginal improvement efforts. Activities at Acheron and Mohican stations emphasised the potential of Aboriginal adults, particularly their adoption of European agriculture. After two years of unsatisfactory progress and expense, the rhetoric of the Central Board shifted to the potential of Aboriginal children. For example, when the *Second Report of the Central Board* announced the selection of a 'better site, on the north side of the River Yarra', the envisaged activities and achievements highlighted by the board were not agricultural; rather 'it is proposed to found a school for the neglected black and half-caste children, and an asylum for infirm blacks'.[41] The report, published in 1862, also listed the many perceived vices of Aboriginal adults, before declaring that it was not 'to be expected, that in two years the Board should have produced any marked change in their condition'. Thus, the board justified a shift from protecting Aboriginal adults to shaping Aboriginal children:

> Without ceasing to hope for their moral improvement, it is our first
> duty to supply them with food and shelter; to protect them as far
> as possible from contact with the debased amongst our own people;
> and to provide instruction for the children, black and half-caste.[42]

Queries brought to the Central Board in the preceding years had drawn attention to the issue of 'orphaned' Aboriginal children.[43] In June 1860, the circumstances of a Taungurung 'orphan' prompted the board to seek power to forcibly remove an Aboriginal child from an 'undesirable' situation. The case concerned a Taungurung child referred to as 'the Young Queen of Benalla Tribe'. This girl was in the custody of a publican in Benalla, a white man named James Banfield. A concerned correspondent wrote to the board recommending the removal of the girl, alarmed that she, like others, was being 'kept by pastoralists and publicans for immoral

---

41 Victoria, Parliament, *Second Report of the Central Board*, 5.
42 Victoria, Parliament, *Second Report of the Central Board*, 15.
43 The designation 'orphan', based upon the absence of biological parents in a nuclear family, overlooked wider kinship responsibilities in Aboriginal child raising.

purposes'.[44] The publican, who was influential in mining circles, was described in the local paper as 'the respected landlord of the Liverpool Arms'.[45] Rather than relinquishing the child, James Banfield requested that the board supply 'a grant of land for her maintenance and education'.[46] When the board met on 30 July 1860 they did not debate the merits of this proposal. They responded instead to a letter from concerned Benalla resident Mrs McKellar who 'earnestly entreated the Board to remove the girl from the house of the Banfields—where she was subject of necessity to the demoralising influences of Hotel life'.[47] The board was uncertain of its power to forcibly take the child from her 'adopted father'.[48] Advice was promptly sought, as 'the necessity for action was urgent'. Placing the young 'Queen of Benalla' in the Melbourne Orphan Asylum was mooted, but 'a different asylum' was clearly needed 'for native children'. William Thomas, Guardian of Aborigines, was then approached to accept 'charge' of Aboriginal children, and to develop an appropriate scheme.[49] On 20 August 1860, Crown law officers informed the board that they had 'no power to remove the Young Queen of Benalla' or any other Aboriginal children.[50] The board sought immediate legislative change to gain 'full power to order as to the custody of minors (Aboriginals and half-castes) in certain cases'.[51] A letter was sent to Banfield instructing him to 'forward the girl to Melbourne without delay to enable the Board to judge for themselves of her character and education'.[52] Banfield refused, and instead recruited a minister of religion Rev. Piper to advocate for their cause, arguing 'that the Banfields deserved great credit for adopting and educating the girl'.[53] Banfield must have held some influence, as the board did not pursue this case further.

---

44 Barwick, *Rebellion at Coranderrk*, 78.

45 'Snowy River', *Ovens and Murray Advertiser*, 4 Aug 1860, 2.

46 Minute, 25 June 1860, Central Board Appointed to Watch Over the Interests of the Aborigines in the Colony of Victoria, NAA, B314, Item 1, Roll 1.

47 Minute, 30 July 1860, Central Board Appointed to Watch Over the Interests of the Aborigines in the Colony of Victoria, NAA, B314, Item 1, Roll 1.

48 Minute, 25 June 1860, Board Meeting Minutes 1860–1862, NAA, B335/0, Box 1, Folio 4.; Minute, 30 July 1860, Board Meeting Minutes 1860–1862, NAA, B335/0, Box 1, Folio 51.

49 Minute, 30 July 1860, Central Board Appointed to Watch Over the Interests of the Aborigines in the Colony of Victoria, NAA, B314, Item 1, Roll 1.

50 Minute, 20 August 1860, Central Board Appointed to Watch Over the Interests of the Aborigines in the Colony of Victoria, NAA, B314, Roll 1.

51 Minute, 20 August 1860, Central Board Appointed to Watch Over the Interests of the Aborigines in the Colony of Victoria, NAA, B314, Item 1, Roll 1.

52 Minute, 20 August 1860, Central Board Appointed to Watch Over the Interests of the Aborigines in the Colony of Victoria, NAA, B314, Item 1, Roll 1.

53 Minute, 10 September 1860, Central Board Appointed to Watch Over the Interests of the Aborigines in the Colony of Victoria, NAA, B314, Item 1, Roll 1.

However, the board persisted in seeking necessary changes to prevent future defiance of their authority over Aboriginal children. Guardian Thomas was empowered to undertake 'the supervision of Aboriginal children, under the charge of a man and a matron in a proposed refuge'.[54] This role was first performed by the matron at Coranderrk, Mrs Green, in December 1863.[55] The Central Board noted in its fourth report that, 'as soon as the buildings at Coranderrk were finished' and fit for the occupation of children, it would secure:

> Any neglected Aboriginal children amongst the blacks ... who should be maintained and educated by the Board. The letter had reference only to orphans and children who had been abandoned; but it was made known ... that the Central Board would be willing to take charge of any children surrendered to them by the Aborigines themselves. On enquiry it was found that the blacks are reluctant to give up their children. They are, usually, very kind to their offspring, and they are jealous of any interference with them by the whites.[56]

Given his formative encounters with Wurundjeri family groups, John Green was aware that Aboriginal parenting included the active involvement of a circle of kin. Nevertheless, in the coming years Green used his influence to convince Aboriginal parents to relinquish their children. According to Richard Broome:

> In all, Green brought sixty children to Coranderrk, many given up by their parents voluntarily as he convinced the parents that 'they were better off with me than exposed to strong temptations'. Many parents followed later.[57]

This rationale for removing Aboriginal children was endorsed throughout the colony by 'honorary correspondents' who were authorised to intervene in Aboriginal affairs. Green explained that:

> All the honorary correspondents agree that something ought to be done to rescue the children from growing up in ignorance, and especially the girls, to keep them from a life of infamy.[58]

---

54 Victoria, Parliament, *Fourth Report of the Central Board*, 10.
55 Minute, 20 August 1860, Board Meeting Minutes 1860–1862, NAA, B335/0, Box 1, Folio 27; Victoria, Parliament, *Fourth Report of the Central Board*, 10.
56 Victoria, Parliament, *Fourth Report of the Central Board*, 10.
57 Broome, *Aboriginal Victorians*, 132.
58 Victoria, Parliament, *Sixth Report of the Central Board*, 12.

Richard Broome has suggested that, as general inspector of Aborigines, John Green 'was the most active in gaining new residents for the reserve', bringing Aboriginal people 'from the Goulburn, Jim Crow (Mount Franklin), Sandhurst (Bendigo), the Terricks, the Murray and Echuca'.[59] The 1869 Aborigines Act reformed the Central Board Appointed to Watch Over the Interests of Aborigines, which had been operating in Victoria since 1860, and created a new Central Board for the Protection of Aborigines. These changes finally granted administrators power to forcibly resettle Aboriginal children by order of council.[60] New child residents secured by these administrative changes included Uncle Roy's grandparents. Their experience of childhood at Coranderrk would be increasingly marked by board intervention and Aboriginal 'rebellion at Coranderrk'.[61]

---

59   Broome, *Aboriginal Victorians*, 132.
60   Barwick, 'And the Lubras', 53.
61   See Barwick, *Rebellion at Coranderrk*; Nanni and James, *Coranderrk*.

5

Children of Coranderrk, 1870–86

Uncle Roy Patterson's Dja Dja Wurrung grandfather, John Patterson, and Taungurung grandmother, Lizzie Edmonds, entered the Coranderrk dormitory at the end of a 'golden era' of growth when, between 1863 and 1874, the station had become a 'self-sufficient and self-determinant Aboriginal community'.[1] However, as these children grew up, they experienced the impact of tumultuous change in the management of the station, as the policies of the Central Board for the Protection of Aborigines shifted from protection to assimilation, and the collaborative and caring John Green was replaced by a series of authoritarian and punitive managers. The Aboriginal Natives Protection Bill of 1869, which created the new board, also included a provision to allow the 'governor from time to time to make regulations'. Jane Miller noted that this capacity was 'in many ways more chilling than the Acts', as it 'provided the prescriptive details that shaped so many lives'.[2] Powers to control Aboriginal residence, work, wages and children were enshrined in the 1869 Act, and consolidated by subsequent amendments. These changes undermined Aboriginal independence and divided Aboriginal families according to imposed categorisations of racial heritage or 'caste'. Because John Patterson and Lizzie Edmonds were labelled, in the offensive lexicon of the time, as 'half-castes', their right to refuge at Coranderrk came under challenge.

---

1   Nanni and James, *Coranderrk*, 16.
2   Miller, 'A Guide to Government Acts', 176–77.

Records suggest that John Patterson, Uncle Roy's grandfather, was born at Mount Hope Station in c. 1869, 15 miles (24 km) south of the Murray River on Barababaraba Country in the northern central plains of Victoria. His mother, Emma Kerr, lived on Mount Hope Station and received rations once a week from pastoralist and local Guardian of Aborigines Molesworth Greene, who also owned neighbouring Pyramid Hill stations from 1857 to 1883.[3] According to Greene, seven Aboriginal people were permanently resident on the station, four men and three women and their children lived and worked on the station, 'go[ing] away perhaps for a few days' fishing, but they were, to all intents and purposes, resident; and other members of their tribe used to come occasionally'.[4] Rev. John Green visited Mount Hope Station in July 1870 and, seeing three 'half-caste women, 1 half-caste lad, and 5 children', tried to convince them to move to Coranderrk:

> They all seemed willing to come when I spoke to them about going the night I arrived, but next morning they were all gone (hid) ... I found them during the day among the rocks ... now they were not willing to go without one man (Sam), who was not there. I stayed all night again, hoping to induce them to go with me, but in the morning they were not to be found. I think some of the white men who cohabit with them assisted them to get away. I left notice with Mr. Greene to write to the Central Board when they came back with Sam, and that I would return and take them.[5]

Molesworth Greene also held the view that the young women were in moral danger on the station, so the group were eventually 'sent off to Coranderrk'. The pastoralist noted that the families left reluctantly, refusing to be separated:

> I should have liked to have kept the men, but they would all go together. I had a great difficulty in getting them to go at all. I know that some of the half-caste women were living with some of the stockmen, and I had a great difficulty to get them away. Mr Green, of the mission station, came and helped me.[6]

---

3   Billis and Kenyon, *Pastoral Pioneers*, 61.
4   Molesworth Greene, minutes of evidence 1531, 25 May 1877, in Victoria, *Report of the Commissioners*, 56.
5   John Green, report, 16 July 1870, in Victoria, Parliament, *Seventh Report of the Board*, Appendix 1, 5.
6   Molesworth Greene, minutes of evidence 1531, 25 May 1877, in Victoria, *Report of the Commissioners*, 56.

Rev. Green admitted to the 1877 inquiry that the Aboriginal women did not leave Mount Hope voluntarily. Asked whether coercion had been used in any case, he replied:

> Two or three women at Mount Hope; a little was used there. Mr Greene, a settler, wanted them taken away, because they were living as common prostitutes amongst his men.[7]

Molesworth Greene's assessment of the situation on Mount Hope included an observation that sexual propriety was culturally contingent:

> I do not think that the natives themselves feel the immorality as European women feel it. It does not degrade them as it does Europeans ... they do not lose their self-respect.[8]

Yet, Greene took steps to bring an end to cross-racial cohabitation, claiming that it was debasing and 'a bad thing for the station'.[9] This may have been in response to external pressures, including from Christian circles, where information about settler Australia had long focused on the abuse of Aboriginal women and children. Stations like Mount Hope were represented as 'sites of peculiarly unchecked white male sin ... as men indulged in unrestrained appetites to have sex, to exploit resources and to kill'.[10] As Elizabeth Elbourne has argued, only 'Christian men' like pastoralist Molesworth Greene and Rev. John Green 'stood between such undomesticated men and their female victim'.[11]

When this pastoralist and Aboriginal protector conspired to remove Emma Kerr and her children from Mount Hope, Emma was in a relationship with Alick Campbell (1851–c. 1933), a young Barababaraba man who was reared on nearby Gannawarra Station.[12] Although Alick Campbell was content working on Gannawarra for pastoralist Charles Brown Fisher, he 'came in' to Coranderrk 'of his own accord', because he wanted to marry Emma Kerr. Campbell testified in 1877 that he had wished to return to Gannawarra after his marriage, arguing: 'I was fourteen or fifteen years with him [Fisher]—brought up with him ... [but Rev. Green] would

---

7 John Green, minutes of evidence 2143, in Victoria, *Report of the Commissioners,* 83.

8 Elbourne, 'The Sin of the Settler', n.p.

9 Molesworth Greene, minutes of evidence 1533, 25 May 1877, in Victoria, *Report of the Commissioners,* 56.

10 Elbourne, 'The Sin of the Settler', n.p.

11 Elbourne, 'The Sin of the Settler', n.p.

12 Barwick, *Rebellion at Coranderrk,* 154.

not let me go'.[13] Emma Kerr married Alick Campbell on 15 April 1873, the union witnessed by John Green and his wife Mary, some 16 months before John Green's forced resignation from his post as manager.[14] Alick Campbell, his new wife Emma Kerr and her children John and Jane Patterson remained at Coranderrk, and the dormitory became their home for the next 16 years.

John Patterson appears in the records again in 1877, when his stepfather, Alick Campbell, reported to a government inquiry into the Aborigines of Victoria that eight-year-old John attended school at Coranderrk. This inquiry marks the culmination of protests by Aboriginal residents, including the Campbells, who played 'a shrewd political game' using petitions, letters and deputations to force a review of deteriorating conditions on the station.[15] The settlement had been described as 'virtually self-supporting' by 1875, with over 1,200 hectares cleared for vegetables and grain crops, over 4 miles (7 km) of land fenced, and 32 cottages and outbuildings constructed. Aboriginal farmers also produced award-winning hops that attracted high market prices, yet the future of the settlement was very unsure. There was no security of title and neighbouring farmers clamoured to close the station.[16]

Uncle Roy's grandmother, Lizzie Edmonds (also spelt Edmunds), entered the Coranderrk records in 1876, during this period of conflict and instability. Lizzie was six years old and resident in the dormitory with three siblings: Lilly (nine), Willie (seven) and Lucy (three). Lizzie's mother and father, William and Lydia Edmonds, also gain mention in the board's report of 1876, as does six-day-old baby Murdock Edmonds, who died of a chest cold in July. Lizzie Edmonds was born in 1869, near Wangaratta (probably at Wahgunyah), before the family moved to Coranderrk.[17] Northern Taungurung clans had alliances with Bangerang and Kwatkwat clans on the Murray River, links that enabled kin to take refuge at Lake Moodemere, an Aboriginal reserve near Wahgunyah.[18] The relocation of the Edmonds family to Coranderrk perhaps reflects the influence of

---

13   Alexander Campbell, minutes of evidence 728–36, in Victoria, *Report of the Commissioners*, 28.
14   See Barwick, *Rebellion at Coranderrk*, Ch. 6.
15   Furphy, *Edward M. Curr*, 134.
16   Balint et al., 'The "Minutes of Evidence" Project', 209.
17   Records detail Elizabeth Edmonds birth place as 'Nagunyah', this is likely a misspelling of 'Wahgunyah'. Family history places her birth as 'near Wangaratta'. The Lake Moodemere Aboriginal reserve, near Wahgunyah, was situated 25 miles (40 km) from Wangaratta near the Murray River.
18   Barwick, *Rebellion at Coranderrk*, 263.

Thomas Bamfield, clan head of the Yeeun-illam-balluk (the northernmost Taungurung clan) after the closure of Mohican Station. Bamfield gathered the 'survivors of his clan' to Coranderrk Station and then played a key leadership role in political efforts to prevent closure of the new settlement.[19] For example, Bamfield wrote to the board in July 1881, seeking the transfer of 'children in Wangaratta belonging to my people'.[20] He gained the attention of the board by renewing allegations that local publicans kept Aboriginal children for immoral purposes:

> Please I trouble you about them children in Wangaratta near Benalla belonging to my people belonging to my brother children and they starving … and they got no place to stop in and I like to bring them over into this school half a [dozen] children in Wangaratta … if you can oblige a pass for us three to fetch them all in Coranderrk I will be very thankful. I had a letter from them some weeks ago and I give the letter to Mr [Strickland] I don't think he give it to you … they get no clothes and nobody to look after them. My brother sold one of the girls to the publican for five bottles of grog if you give me authority to take that girl away from the publican to put it in the police hand to fetch them up here if you can oblige me so much money for my letter if you please.[21]

Bamfield's appeal was quickly dismissed by the local guardian of Aborigines at Wangaratta, Alexander Tone, who retorted:

> There is not one particle of truth in his statement that any children are starving here neither are there any girls sold to a publican. The Aboriginals here have been contented and when I ask them if any desired to go and live at Coranderrk they exclaimed 'No fear that place too cold'. In fact, the two who knew [Coranderrk] told me some time ago that they would not go back, they like Wangaratta which they call their own country … it strikes me Mr Bamfield wants a trip on the cheap.[22]

Tone positioned Bamfield as a lying opportunist. This slander is unsurprising, given that Bamfield was a key Aboriginal activist on Coranderrk. His actions had embarrassed the board, which targeted him

---

19   Barwick, 'Mapping the Past', 128; Nanni and James, *Coranderrk*, 73.
20   Thomas Bamfield to Captain Page, n.d, Central Board for the Protection of Aborigines, Correspondence Files 1869–1957, NAA, B313, Item 42, Folio 19.
21   Thomas Bamfield to Captain Page, n.d, Central Board for the Protection of Aborigines, Correspondence Files 1869–1957, NAA, B313, Item 42, Folio 19.
22   Alexander Tone, Wangaratta, to Captain Page, 30 July 1881, Central Board for the Protection of Aborigines, Correspondence Files 1869–1957, NAA, B313, Item 42, Folio 20.

with increasing and punitive vilification.[23] Tone also revealed that he had consulted Yorta Yorta people for their views on Coranderrk: people who naturally favoured continuing on 'their own country' at Wangaratta over residence on Kulin land.

'A most astonishing thing on the part of the manager': Suppression on Coranderrk

Another outcome for the children of Coranderrk during these tumultuous years, particularly after the resignation of John Green, was the suppression of cultural activities under the authority of the four 'uncaring managers' who replaced him.[24] Uncle Roy recalls the management of Rev. Frederick Strickland (1878–82) as particularly oppressive:

> What happened was the Church of England Minister stopped them from teaching their culture, their Dreamtime, their spirit world, their language, and destroyed their being. If they were caught teaching it, they were bullwhipped or gaoled or both, so it wasn't a very good life for the Aboriginal people in them days. It might have been because of that we lost our language and our way of life. In my opinion, they took our being away from us.[25]

Managers usurped the authority of Aboriginal Elders in religious matters and supressed cultural activity because they believed it undermined the Christian civilising agenda of the station. Aboriginal Elders took extreme care to disguise their efforts to teach traditional knowledge to younger generations, as 'it was against the law' of the station.[26] Uncle Roy recalls that his grandparents remained cautious long after the closure of Coranderrk:

> When I grew up, I wanted to learn about culture from my grandmother and grandfather. So, me grandmother'd be walking around the flats down there in Healesville, grandfather had a big long tea-tree pole that had a string on it, makin' out that we were fishing. If anyone came along, he put out the pole and made out

---

23 Nanni and James, *Coranderrk*, 203, 73.
24 Broome, *Aboriginal Victorians*, 169.
25 Roy Patterson, in conversation with Jennifer Jones, 3 March 2016, DS3001137.
26 Roy Patterson, in conversation with Jennifer Jones, 3 March 2016, DS3001137.

that we were fishing. You can pick up some dry cow manure and get the worms from under it and put them in a tin. That was our bait. So, while I was down there, and we were makin' out that we were fishing, my grandmother was telling culture and Dreamtime.[27]

Aboriginal residents learnt the value of discretion under the punitive managers of Coranderrk and ensured that their children and grandchildren observed the same caution. Rev. John Green showed a degree of respect and understanding for Aboriginal culture, but Rev. Strickland was perceived to be disdainful of Aboriginal tradition and 'cold and distant' with residents. John Green also offered much appreciated medical expertise to the sick, as well as spiritual succour via his Presbyterian rituals.[28] An inquiry into Coranderrk Aboriginal Station in 1881 heard complaints that Rev. Strickland was both self-interested and neglectful of Aboriginal health. When Emma Campbell, Uncle Roy's great-grandmother, was ill and in need of hospitalisation, Strickland refused assistance. On 30 September 1881, Alick Campbell told the inquiry that:

> When I asked him for the buggy to take my wife to Melbourne—she was sick with rheumatic fever—he said no, I could not have the buggy because he wanted it for his own use, to drive the family to the Black Spur; and when I was going away I asked him for money. I said, 'Will you give me some money to go down to town?' He said 'No, I have got no money.' I said, 'have you not got any Government money?' He said, 'No, I have not.' I said, 'How am I to do?' He said, 'I do not know.' So I borrowed some money from the people round about here, and took my wife down [to hospital, where Emma was admitted for three weeks].[29]

Grievances against Strickland led five members of the Campbell family—Alick, Emma, their daughter Jane and son John Patterson, and Emma's younger brother Phinnimore Jackson—to sign a community petition on 16 November 1881, demanding Strickland's resignation.[30] A total of 46 Aboriginal signatories called for increased independence:

---

27 Roy Patterson, in conversation with Jennifer Jones, 3 March 2016, DS3001137.

28 Barwick, *Rebellion at Coranderrk*, 116; Broome, *Aboriginal Victorians*, 172.

29 Victoria, Parliament, *Report of the Board*, 19.

30 Petition, 16 November 1881, in Victoria, Parliament, *Report of the Board*, 98.

> We want the Board and the Inspector, Captain Page, to be no longer over us. We want only one man here, and that is Mr. John Green, and the station to be under the Chief Secretary [equivalent to today's State Premier]; then we will show the country that the station could self-support itself.[31]

Uncle Roy's great-uncle William Edmond was also a signatory.

William Edmond and Phinnimore Jackson were both aged just 13, yet both had personal motivation to seek Strickland's removal. The boys, along with fellow dormitory inmate Tommy Dick, were beaten by Strickland for attending the horse races at Yarra Flat without his permission on 22 May 1880. Phinnimore Jackson received particularly brutal treatment, because he resisted the thrashing and complained to his sister Emma Campbell about his treatment. He testified at the 1881 inquiry that Strickland:

> Gave me a good thrashing with his hands. He told me he was going for a riding whip so I told him I was going to my sister, to show the bruises that were on my back. So he came over and looked for me, and could not find me. He came to my sister's and asked where I was, and she spoke to him about the whipping I got … He locked the store-room and kept me in there, and put my head between his legs and gave me a thrashing with the bridle reins.[32]

Corporal punishment was accepted as a form of paternal discipline in this period, and Strickland defended his action by arguing that: 'It has been my habit since I have been here of associating myself with [the Aboriginal inmates at Coranderrk] as a brother or a father'. According to Strickland, Phinnimore was disciplined as if 'he had been my own child'.[33]

Yet, Aboriginal adults, including Phinnimore's sister Emma and his brother-in-law Alick Campbell, did not share this interpretation of the beating. When relatives heard about the harsh treatment and incarceration of the children, Jack Briggs, Alick Campbell and Alfred Davis 'demanded to see the boys', and 'each took away a boy in defiance of Mr Strickland', despite his threats to summons them for 'interfering with me in the exercise of my duty'.[34] Strickland persisted in charging five Aboriginal

---

31   Petition, 16 November 1881, in Victoria, Parliament, *Report of the Board*, 98.
32   Minute of evidence 2576, in Victoria, Parliament, *Report of the Board*, 61.
33   Minute of evidence 2589, in Victoria, Parliament, *Report of the Board*, 61.
34   Minute of evidence 2589, in Victoria, Parliament, *Report of the Board*, 61; Minute, Meeting of the Board for the Protection of the Aborigines, 27 May 1880, NAA, B314, Roll 1.

men 'for insubordination', as they had threatened that 'they would take away all the children as they were being knocked about and half killed by Mr Strickland'.[35] Unable to find the police constable in Healesville, the Aboriginal men took Phinnimore Jackson to Rev. Green, who lived nearby, showing him injuries including a deep cut to the head. Green noted his disapproval of Strickland's actions, telling the Coranderrk inquiry that he thought it was:

> Very wrong to prosecute the men for taking the part of the boy who had been so severely chastised … a most astonishing thing on the part of the manager, and a clergyman, to prosecute them for doing a friendly part towards their own children.[36]

Diane Barwick observed that Strickland's control of the children at Coranderrk was then under challenge. Strickland feared that a display of defiance by the men, one of whom angrily 'shook his fist in his face', would foster wider insurrection.[37] He argued in his report to the board that 'the punishment occurred because the dormitory girls were on strike, demanding wages, and had encouraged the boys to rebel'.[38] The board supported Strickland by authorising him, in October 1880, to 'prosecute three parents who refused to let their children go to the Boarding House when so requested by him'.[39] In this way, by resorting to the courts to assert his authority, it is evident that Strickland's management relied upon 'coercion rather than collaboration and consent'.[40]

Training Aboriginal children for 'self-dependence'

Controlling Aboriginal children in the Coranderrk dormitory enabled managers and matrons to exploit their labour and to illustrate the type of social change the government envisaged for Aboriginal society. Much effort was turned towards training children in practical skills, which were

---

35   John Green, minutes of evidence 5084, in Victoria, Parliament, *Report of the Board*, 129; minute, Meeting of the Board for the Protection of the Aborigines, 27 May 1880, NAA, B314, Roll 1.

36   John Green, minutes of evidence 5084, in Victoria, Parliament, *Report of the Board*, 129.

37   Minute, Meeting of the Board for the Protection of the Aborigines, 27 May 1880, NAA, B314, Roll 1.

38   Barwick, *Rebellion at Coranderrk*, 171.

39   Minute, 6 October 1880, Meeting of the Board for the Protection of the Aborigines, NAA, B314, Roll 1.

40   Nanni and James, *Coranderrk*, 138.

thought to show evidence of 'community reform and progress' and 'visible indices of good management'.[41] Academic education was not a priority, as the capability of Aboriginal children was then understood to be limited by their 'race' and 'class'. Only basic religious and practical education was deemed necessary, as this would allay the risk of further moral degeneration.[42] As Amanda Barry has explained, the 1866 commission into compulsory schooling in Victoria determined that there was 'no reason why [the Education Department] should charge ourselves with [Aborigines'] education'. The Board for the Protection of Aborigines was left to supervise the provision of education on Aboriginal stations as they saw fit.[43] This meant that manual work on the station competed with academic lessons. In 1881, for example, it was noted by the Coranderrk teacher that Phinnimore Jackson did not attend school very often because Strickland 'thought he had enough education' and preferred to employ him as a gardener, mailboy and groom, and to chop wood.[44] Mrs Laura Deans attested that Phinnimore:

> Says himself he is over-worked. He is thirteen. Phinnimore goes for the mail, and carts the wood, and chops it for Mr. Strickland; and he gets in the cows of a night, and milks them in the morning-seven or eight cows. He does a great deal of work on the station. He works in the garden besides.[45]

The management of children at Coranderrk, which already focused more heavily upon training than education, was subject to the discretion of the manager. This had been the case since the inception of the dormitory system. As the manager of Coranderrk in 1877, Hugh Halliday, explained, youth on the station had:

> Every opportunity at present of learning everything requisite for employment on a station or a farm, as well as on a hop plantation, which I think is all that is necessary for them to be learned on the station. The school girls are taught to sew and make their own clothes.[46]

---

41   Barwick, 'And the Lubras', 56.
42   Barry, 'Equal to Children of European Origin', 41.4.
43   Barry, 'A Matter of Primary Importance', 172.
44   Minutes of evidence 2540–2547, 17 November 1881, in Victoria, Parliament, *Report of the Board*, 60.
45   Mrs L. Deans, minutes of evidence 3031–3036, 17 November 1881, in Victoria, Parliament, *Report of the Board*, 70.
46   Correspondence no. 35, in Victoria, *Report of the Commissioners,* Appendix C. 112–13.

This skills training prepared the children for 'self-dependence', as the board's General Inspector Christian Ogilvie explained to the 1877 royal commission. Ogilvie sought the gradual introduction of what he described as a system of 'de-centralisation', which would train and then remove Aboriginal youth from the stations of Victoria. In his proposed scheme:

> Adults should be encouraged to … leave the stations in search of work. And that it should be compulsory on the youth of both sexes that they should be apprenticed to responsible masters and mistresses immediately after their education was completed.[47]

By making Aboriginal people labour 'for themselves', Ogilvie sought to disperse troublemakers and to achieve assimilation through 'eventually absorb[ing] [them] into the general population'.[48]

For the dormitory girls, activities deemed necessary for assimilation included sewing, cooking and housekeeping, along with menial farm work that supported the economic program of the station. Aboriginal women and girls used their skills in gardening and fishing to enable subsistence. They were also active in the harvest of cash crops, including hops, which were under 'extensive and profitable production … at Coranderrk', thus providing additional sources of income for the station.[49] In January–March 1885, Lizzie Edmonds, aged around 16 years, was undertaking 'housework' and 'kitchen duties' in the dormitory—traditional roles assigned to women and signifiers of gender appropriate behaviour. Lizzie Edmonds' disappointing performance of womanly tasks was noted. Lizzie's bad behaviour disrupted the matron's overbearing control and caused much trouble and anxiety. Lizzie was twice noted as 'working well', but was also observed as being 'bad tempered', 'very troublesome' and causing 'much anxiety'. Her behaviour improved in February 1885 and was deemed 'more satisfactory' until the week of 28 February when she was again working in the kitchen. Lizzie was 'disappointed at not receiving wages promised' and, after this breach of trust, seemed 'very troublesome' when expected to work for free.

---

47 Minutes of evidence in Victoria, *Report of the Commissioners*, 1.
48 Broome, *Aboriginal Victorians*, 180.
49 Victoria, *Report of the Commissioners*, x; Barwick, 'And the Lubras', 54–55.

The final note on Lizzie Edmonds' life on Coranderrk, in the week ending 15 March 1885, was that she was engaged out of doors, hop picking, and was 'working well' with the other girls.[50] Each week the 'Returns of Children in Dormitory Coranderrk' noted the name, date, age, colour and employment of the children in the dormitory, along with the remarks of the matron. Under the category 'colour', Lizzie Edmonds was repeatedly described as being a 'half-caste', a designation that would soon result in her expulsion from the station.

'Hiring out half castes': The Board seeks reprisal

Since the establishment of Coranderrk, Aboriginal men, women and children had undertaken a decades-long campaign of protest in the form of strikes, petitions, deputations and testimony, asserting their independence and to claim permanent tenure of the station. Alick Campbell had testified in September 1881 that he and his family wanted to remain at Coranderrk, but that grievances against Strickland's management, as evidenced by the neglect of his wife Emma and harsh treatment of his brother-in-law Phinnimore Jackson, had prompted family protests.[51] Testimonies given by the Aboriginal complainants caused 'deep embarrassment' to the board and its managers. Such evidence also made the brave witnesses vulnerable to retaliatory action.

One avenue available to the board to punish refractory individuals was to banish them from the station.[52] Some months prior to the 1881 inquiry, the board investigated the possible systematisation of expulsion, based on caste. Aboriginal people of mixed descent would be required to 'labor for themselves' in the general community, rather than working for their Aboriginal community on a station.[53] The board identified 'several half castes' living on Coranderrk who 'were quite capable of earning a living outside and recommended that they should be sent away from the

---

50 'Return of Children in Dormitory Coranderrk 1885', Central Board for the Protection of Aborigines, Correspondence Files 1869–1957, NAA, B313, Folios 34–40.

51 Alick Campbell, minutes of evidence 934–49, 30 September 1881, in Victoria, Parliament, *Report of the Board*, 19–20.

52 Regarding the banishment of Thomas Bamfield, see Barwick, *Rebellion at Coranderrk*, 263.

53 Minutes of evidence, 24 April 1877, in Victoria, *Report of the Commissioners*, 1.

station'.[54] In July 1881, after consulting Chief Secretary Berry, the board 'decided to carry out their proposals and remove three men and their wives without delay. The children would be allowed to remain if the parents wished'.[55] Certificates were issued to enable these men to work outside the Aboriginal station, and the board's decision was communicated to the manager, Strickland. The three couples targeted for eviction, all viewed as troublemakers, included Alick Campbell and his wife Emma.[56]

The board's sensitivity to criticism, and its capacity for retaliation, was also illustrated by a response to disparaging statements made about the board in 1881. A white employee at the station, farm overseer William Harris, had questioned managerial oversight and farm viability at the 1881 inquiry. His views were subsequently published in *The Argus*.[57] 'As these statements were quite untrue' in the opinion of the secretary of the board, a special meeting was called on 20 October 1881 and Harris was required 'to give an explanation'.[58] In defending his statements, which centred upon inadequate fencing, Harris also attributed the numbers of trespassing stock to the failure of Aboriginal stockmen, including Alick Campbell. He argued that one former stockman 'would spend a good deal of his time when supposed to be at work at Mrs Malloy's', and that 'Alick Campbell had also been stockman and found unsatisfactory'.[59] Despite these slurs, both Campbell and his workmate were identified as capable of independence and exiled into the white community. Alick Campbell gained work on a pastoral station but was 'barely making a living' in late 1884 when the family requested permission to return to Coranderrk to 'give the children schooling'.[60] The family's reprieve from the board's new dispersal policy was, however, short lived.

---

54   Minute, 1 June 1881, Meeting of the Board for the Protection of the Aborigines, NAA, B314, Roll 1, 386–87.

55   The reply received from Berry was determined to be 'not so satisfactory as the Board could desire', but they 'decided to carry out their proposals and remove three men and their wives without delay'. Minute, 6 July 1881, Meeting of the Board for the Protection of the Aborigines, NAA, B314, Roll 1, 387–88.

56   Barwick, *Rebellion at Coranderrk*, 287. These removals presumably took place after Campbell's testimony at the inquiry in September 1881 and before Strickland resigned in February 1882. Minute, 1 February 1882, Meeting of the Board for the Protection of the Aborigines, NAA, B314, Roll 1, 375.

57   'The Coranderrk Inquiry', *The Argus*, 19 October 1881, 6.

58   Minute, 20 October 1881, Meeting of the Board for the Protection of the Aborigines, NAA, B314, Roll 1, 390.

59   Minute, 15 November 1881, Meeting of the Board for the Protection of the Aborigines, NAA, B314, Roll 1, 392.

60   Barwick, *Rebellion at Coranderrk*, 287.

While the Campbell family were struggling in exile, the board designed legislation to evict all individuals and families of mixed racial descent from government stations. Not all officials supported the scheme. In March 1883, the board received a letter from the chief secretary asking the board to 'reconsider its decision':

> On the matter of hiring out half castes and quadroons. Some discussion took place but the meeting did not alter its previous opinion. The secretary was to reply to the effect that the meeting was of the opinion that half caste married couples should be encouraged to go to service and also half caste youths.[61]

Subsequent correspondence and discussion in April 1883 centred upon the moral dangers such placements might pose. Some members of the board were strongly opposed to 'hiring out' girls, but preparations to enact the amendments continued regardless. In March 1884, the managers of Aboriginal stations in Victoria were questioned regarding the number and ages of youths capable of being apprenticed out, and the financial and 'practical effect of withdrawing such labour from the stations'.[62] In May 1884, the board had revised their draft regulations 'for merging half castes' and resolved to lay the resolutions before the chief secretary. The amendments to the Act, which were to take effect on 1 January 1885, set out a detailed seven-year timetable for the assimilation of Aboriginal people of mixed descent over the age of 13 years. Assistance and amelioration would be gradually withdrawn as 'the process of merging should be complete as soon as possible, after which all responsibility of the Government as regards them would cease—*finality* being thus attained'.[63]

'Finality', according to the board, meant that the impacted Aboriginal adults would 'be accounted in all respects free and equal citizens of the colony' and Aboriginal children would:

> From the earliest period of their recollection … be accustomed to regard themselves as members of the community at large, and may not be constrained to carry with them through life the impressions of the indolent habits and manners of their original black friends.[64]

---

61   Minute, 7 March 1883, Meeting of the Board for the Protection of the Aborigines, NAA, B314, Roll 1, 422.

62   Minute, 5 March 1884, Meeting of the Board for the Protection of the Aborigines, NAA, B314, Roll 1, 439.

63   Minute, 1 May 1884, Meeting of the Board for the Protection of the Aborigines, NAA, B314, Roll 1, 445.

64   Minute, 1 May 1884, Meeting of the Board for the Protection of the Aborigines, NAA, B314, Roll 1, 445.

The board thus sought an end to financial impost on government, and to ensure the generational loss of Aboriginal culture and identity via assimilation into the 'community at large'. As Uncle Roy observes:

> Every tribe that went on Coranderrk, they tried to take their laws off them, their culture off them, their Dreamtime off them, everything. They had to learn the white people's way and when the kids grew up, they never had their language or nothin'.[65]

The Aborigines Protection Act, passed on 16 December 1886, led to the exile of 50 Aboriginal people of mixed descent from Coranderrk. Diane Barwick recorded that the majority went to Maloga Mission, receiving welcome in New South Wales thanks to clan ties in the Murray district. When Maloga Mission closed, these people relocated to a new government station, Cummeragunja. John Patterson and Lizzie Edmonds, the young couple who had grown up together at Coranderrk, were among these refugees. They married at Cummeragunja on New Year's Day in 1891, both aged 22. Witnesses to the marriage, Willie Edmonds and Jane Patterson, were siblings of the bride and groom, suggesting that both extended families had joined the 'influx of Coranderrk people' that 'began in 1884 after the new Act for "dispersing" half-castes and merging them with the general population was mooted, and became law in 1886'.[66] Forced from their home and into exile in New South Wales, the Coranderrk refugees were perceived by Maloga missionary Daniel Matthews as 'sometimes insolent' and willing to 'defy any authority'.[67] Nancy Cato characterised the migrants as 'the strongest willed, most vocal and disaffected' of Aboriginal people, who 'hated coercion'.[68] This independent spirit, combined with obligations back in Victoria, saw many Coranderrk families choose to return to the Healesville district. John and Lizzie Patterson, for example, had their first two children, Alexander and Lilian, at Cummeragunja in 1893. However, their third child, Thelma, was born at Coranderrk in 1895. The family returned to live near the old station, despite being 'ineligible for aid or residence', and 'descendants of the pioneers—the Davis, Franklin, Harris, Hunter, Manton, Patterson, Rowan, Russell, Terrick and Wandin families ... camped in huts and tents to be near their "old people"'.[69]

---

65   Roy Patterson, in conversation with Jennifer Jones, 3 March 2016, DS3001137.
66   Cato, *Mr Maloga*, 207.
67   Cato, *Mr Maloga*, 235.
68   Barwick, *Rebellion at Coranderrk*, 207.
69   Barwick, *Rebellion at Coranderrk*, 304.

This return to the Healesville district coincided with the development of a large-scale sawmilling industry in the eastern forests. The extension of the Victorian railways system to Healesville in 1889 saw the town develop as a railhead for a relatively stable local timber industry.[70] Healesville businessman and local identity Thomas Crowley opened a number of sawmills in the surrounding district after 1891, building a tramway to his Myers Creek mill and branch lines through the bush to reach remote timber.[71] These timber enterprises and associated developments brought employment to the district. John Patterson gained reliable work in the timber industry, and the Patterson family made a permanent home at the Coranderrk Village Settlement, an '80 acre block of land outside the reserve fence'.[72] Here they celebrated the births of Henry in 1898, Lydia in 1900 and Doris in 1902. John and Lizzie Patterson's youngest child, Frank Patterson (Uncle Roy's father), was born in Healesville in 1911. Family stability was made possible by local work opportunities and John Patterson's work ethic. As Uncle Roy recalled:

> Me grandfather, he was a worker … He was working hard fellin' the trees and bring the logs up with the draught horses. Me grandfather cut a lot of timber for the railway line between Healesville and Yarra Glen; with an axe and the old crosscut saw, a six-foot crosscut saw, five-pound plumb axe, hammer and big steel tree wedge. They brought the timber out by horse and dray, took it down to Healesville and then put it on the railway line. Me grandfather taught dad how to work timber, that was our way of life. The work was there, so they wouldn't go any further; that is why I grew up in Healesville.[73]

Uncle Roy's family chose to remain at Healesville after Coranderrk closed as an Aboriginal reserve in February 1924 and remaining residents were transferred to Lake Tyres, Gippsland.[74] He explained:

> My grandfather and father, uncles and aunties wouldn't go down there because their work was in Healesville. My grandfather said, 'I'm workin' here, my life is here … I am not going down

---

70 Lennon, 'Wrecks and Ruins'.
71 Symonds, *Healesville*, 86.
72 Barwick, *Rebellion at Coranderrk*, 310.
73 Roy Patterson, in conversation with Jennifer Jones, 3 March 2016, DS3001137.
74 Barwick, *Rebellion at Coranderrk*, 310.

there'. My grandmother said, 'I'm not going down when my family is here, my husband is here, and the children are here. We stay here.'[75]

Uncle Roy joined his father, uncles and brothers in the timber industry after completing his primary education:

> One day my father said, 'How old are you Roy?' I said, 'I'm 14, why dad?' He said, 'Bring your schoolbooks home, you start work Monday'. So, I bought me schoolbooks home and Saturday he gave me an axe and he showed me how to sharpen it; it took me two days and I still couldn't do it properly; me father had to finish it off. My Uncle Henry, he taught me how to sharpen saws; taught me to use the circular saw, crosscut saw, hand saw. I used to be one of the best chainsaw operators around. I started working up the forest with my father, me eldest brother worked with dad and me. My other brothers worked in the timber mill. Dad used to drive us out; leave home at five o'clock in the morning and get back at half past six/seven at night, six days a week. I got 4/10- a week ($9). Dad kept the £4 and give me 10 bob pocket money. In 1957, my father was killed. A tree come over the back of the dozer and hit him on the head and killed him. I was only 16. I was one of 10 children, born in the middle. When he was killed, I went into the sawmill and started as a rouseabout; pickin' up all the rubbish timber that was cut and throwin' it on the fire. Then I went what they call 'tailing out', at the back of the saw. I went to number one benchman, cutting the timber, running it through the saw.[76]

This generational teamwork in the forests and mills not only supported the family financially, but also provided opportunity for Elders to pass down traditional knowledge and bush skills. As Uncle Roy recalls:

> My grandfather taught me how to track; taught me what the animal was, to only hunt food enough to take home. When you go out to hunt you have to remember what the Elders taught ya; how to camouflage yourself by putting mud over ya to keep your odour away from the animal. When the kangaroos and emus can't smell ya, it's because of the mud. He taught me how to make

---

75   Barwick, *Rebellion at Coranderrk*, 310.
76   Roy Patterson, in conversation with Jennifer Jones, 3 March 2016, DS3001137.

a weapon; that craft has gone now because me hands are no good. The vibration of chainsaws, hammers, axes and the hard work I done all me life buggered that hand up and the shoulder.[77]

The physical demands of forest and mill work punished Uncle Roy's body, but such labour also gave him access to the bush and opportunity to learn from his Elders. This knowledge informs the next two chapters and motivated the writing of this book.

77   Roy Patterson, in conversation with Jennifer Jones, 3 March 2016, DS3001137.

PART 2: SHARING TAUNGURUNG CULTURE

6

'Knowledge cost ya nothing and is not heavy to carry around': Taungurung bush tucker, bush medicine and bushcraft

Uncle Roy held a deep respect for both his grandparents, but a special bond with his grandmother gave him authority as a Taungurung Elder and teacher. At the end of her life, Lizzie Edmond Patterson entrusted young Roy with spiritual custodianship:

> On the 12th of February 1950, when I was 9½ years old, dad came and picked me up out of school and took me down to my grandparents' place. Grandfather grabbed me and took me into the bedroom where Nanna was. She was still in bed, and grandfather put me in the bed beside my grandmother. She put her arms around me, and I put my arm around her, and my grandfather went to the other side of the room. I don't know how long I was there, but after a while grandfather come over and took Nanna's arm off me and took my arm off her and walked me outside. He give me to my mother, and then walked back into the bedroom. A little while later he said 'he's got his grandmother's spirit'. Nanna told

me about respect, and when she died she gave me her spirit. That was quite a few days ago now. I am proud of it and she is still there today; she is still there within me and she guides me.[1]

This responsibility or mantle, passed from grandmother to grandchild, undergirded Uncle Roy's desire to teach Taungurung history and culture. After our initial meetings, Uncle Roy commented:

> I think first we better go up to that bush tucker mob and spend some time up there, so you can actually taste it and feel it firsthand; this is going to open up your eyes darl, I mean it. You see, people think, 'Oh, that's only a weed', but you wait until you *taste* that weed, it is unreal. I'm goin' to talk about the bush tucker, which I learnt through my grandmother and grandfather mainly. I wasn't very old when it started up, only about 4 or 5 years old.[2]

Uncle Roy makes the important point that plants growing 'wild' in the bush might be mistaken as weeds by the uninformed, but this misnaming does not affect the importance of the plant as tucker. Defining what is or is not a weed is culturally contingent; human–plant interactions are directly influenced by social conceptualisations of vegetation.[3] Since invasion, the attitudes of European settlers to indigenous vegetation has been shaped by utilitarian, psychological and aesthetic considerations.[4] A preference for open country, neatly tilled fields and familiar European species influenced what Tom Griffiths has described as 'century-scale vegetation change' in Australia.[5] When Uncle Roy saw introduced species like poplars and willows growing uncontrolled in the bush, he commented that Europeans brought them over to Australia so that they could feel more at home. He asked: 'Why didn't they just stay at home and appreciate them over there?'

---

1   Roy Patterson, in conversation with Jennifer Jones, 3 March 2016, DS3001137.
2   Roy Patterson, in conversation with Jennifer Jones, 3 March 2016, DS3001139.
3   Head and Atchison, 'Cultural Ecology'.
4   Bonyhady, *The Colonial Earth*, 78.
5   Griffiths, 'How Many Trees', 375.

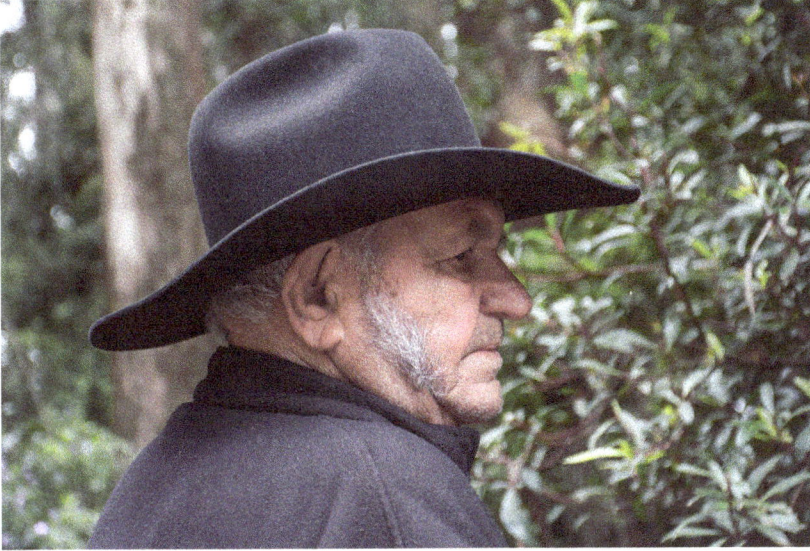

Uncle Roy Patterson
Source: Photographed by Moorina Bonini.

European attitudes to foraging were also shaped by historic perceptions that sedentary agriculture was progressive and advanced, while hunter-gatherer societies were unproblematically viewed as backward or primitive.[6] From this perspective, systematic Aboriginal travel commonly described by the term 'walkabout' was seen as aimless wandering rather than purposeful, systematised and sustainable travel around Country that enabled seasonal management of grains and food plants.[7] As Indigenous environmental management strategies and systems were not considered to be 'farming', they were dismissed, and existing flora was seen as 'an impediment rather than a resource'. Indigenous plants were removed and replaced in a process described as 'improvement'.[8] Contemporary non-Indigenous Australian attitudes to plants could be understood as overlaying ancient and continuing Indigenous Australian cultural relationships with food and medical vegetation. Uncle Roy wanted his readers to become sensitive to this context, recognising that development of respectful attitudes will benefit the coexistence of Aboriginal and non-Aboriginal people on the lands they share.

6   Yen, 'The Domestication of Environment'.
7   Kneebone, 'Interpreting Traditional Culture'; Pascoe, *Dark Emu*.
8   Griffiths, 'How Many Trees', 378.

The first step towards achieving this understanding was to get into the bush, visiting specific local places at the right time and with the right attitude. Uncle Roy's approach to teaching and learning was process and relationship oriented, rather than focused on an endpoint or outcome.[9] He took Moorina Bonini, our photographer, and me onto Country so that our learning was experiential and built upon what we already knew. He was always asking us, 'So, what do you want to know?', and helping us to contextualise new experiences by connecting past with present and future.

We set out to our classroom in the rolling hills, river flats and roadside scrub. The stories Uncle Roy shared about bush tucker and bush medicine were intergenerational, emerging from long family relationships with particular places:[10]

> On Friday night me grandmother and grandfather come and picked me up from home in the horse and dray. They had a big blue draught horse whose name was Jess. Grandfather never had to hit her or nothing; he'd just say 'shake a leg Jess' and she'd get into a trot. They'd take me down to their place at the end of McGretton's Road in Healesville, and then next day me grandfather and I'd go out with the old tea-tree pole with a piece of string, makin out that we are fishin', and me grandfather is teachin' me. A man cannot teach a woman or a girl, and a woman can't teach a man or a boy; that is our law. That's how I learnt my culture and my Dreamtime, about the spirit world and our law; with me Granddad.[11]

As I accompanied Uncle Roy onto Taungurung Country for the first time, he explained that these gender restrictions did not apply to me, because I am non-Aboriginal. I was certainly aware that I was a rookie. Perched uncomfortably in a new university 4WD, I thought I was creeping along the tracks, concentrating on the potholes, when Uncle Roy would interrupt with an urgent 'slow down, slow down'. Hardly 100 metres past the last cleared paddock, and we were already surrounded by bush tucker and bush medicine.

Uncle Roy came alive in the bush. Alert and attentive, he identified distant specimens for us to find and examine. We were in and out of the car to note the form and texture of plants, to crush, smell and taste.

---

9   Acton et al., 'Conversations on Cultural Sustainability'.
10   Tuck, McKenzie and McCoy, 'Land Education', 8.
11   Roy Patterson, in conversation with Jennifer Jones, 3 March 2016, DS3001139.

Uncle Roy's spirit was tireless, but he still had to drag his body in and out of the vehicle. 'Come on you bugger', he would say as he heaved his left leg back into the car again. Moorina and I tried to help, but our efforts were not always welcome.

One time, Uncle Roy spotted the fresh new leaves of a gum tree, up high in a clearing. We headed up the track and pulled the 4WD in as close as possible. It was difficult terrain. Uncle Roy was out of the car in a flash, and soon tumbling down the hill. Thankfully, an embankment of leaves and bark buffered his fall. Moorina and I were still in shock, as Uncle Roy was brushing dirt from his trousers. Back on task, he looked nonplussed and then annoyed as we fussed over him. He had taken harder falls in his life and wanted us to focus on the next lesson. He continued:

> Everything you eat is medicine in our bush tucker; we heal ourselves with what we eat. You can't get nothing better than that. You watch the birds and the animals; what they eat, you can eat. We've got medicine to cure the colds and flu, and it is so simple, it is too easy; but the Europeans have found out about some of our medicine and they are strippin' the trees of it and we get nothing for it. It is our traditional knowledge; most of your medicine in the chemist shop has come from Indigenous knowledge. People say, 'these are only plants!' but they are our food and medicine.[12]

Bush medicine makes use of plants that are abundant in the everyday contexts. Such knowledge has the potential to connect local communities to their natural environments, and to promote respect for local Indigenous people.[13]

In this chapter, Uncle Roy talks about bush medicines that treat a range of ailments, including colds, sore muscles, wounds, headaches and rashes. Uncle Roy treated people in the Taggerty district who came to him for cures. This was his contribution to reconciliation processes:

> I do smoking ceremonies for cleansing your spirit. I don't care what colour skin you got; you've got an inner spirit. The smoking is to cleanse and ease the pain of the hurt within the inner spirit. It doesn't cure it, but it does make it easier to live with the hurt. I've got three people that come up every year for smoking. One of

---

12 Roy Patterson, in conversation with Jennifer Jones, 15 April 2016, DS300143.
13 Ralph-Flint, 'Cultural Borrowing'.

them is an American lady who sent me a letter from America when her mother was dying; she asked me to send a smoking over. I faced north-west and blew the smoke that way. About a month later, she come home and said she could smell the eucalyptus, and when she smelt that, she saw her mother relax; then she died peacefully.[14]

Uncle Roy viewed 'medical pluralism', or the integration of traditional medical practices with biomedical healthcare, as essential to the preservation of Taungurung culture. Improvements in Indigenous and non-Indigenous health and wellbeing come through connection to Country and culture.[15] Bush tucker and bush medicine provide a site where 'Indigenous and non-Indigenous worlds of knowledge and experience' can intersect for the benefit of both people and Country.[16]

Animals also provide Taungurung people and newcomers with guidance in our shared environment. Not all views of the world are secular and/or functional, and Uncle Roy wanted to communicate Taungurung understandings that non-human species and their environments should be held with loving regard:[17]

> The Dreaming comes into everything, our dancing and corroboree, our walkabout, every part of our lives. My totem is the crow; he is a messenger. The koala, he don't drink water; so we go to the koala to get permission to get good water on our walkabout. If we don't ask for permission, we get bad water. That way, we live in the Dreamtime world as a part of daily life; I still live it today. When I am teaching, I am teaching my Dreaming and through the Dreaming we learn the ways of Mother Earth, the ways of Bunjil and the ways of our people.[18]

Uncle Roy's relationship with Bunjil the eagle had an ecological dimension. Bleakley explained this by noting that human–animal relationships provide 'a focus for a wider explicit sympathy with the world at large'.[19] Uncle Roy understood that there is a continuity between humans, animals and the world:

---

14   Roy Patterson, in conversation with Jennifer Jones, 3 March 2016, DS3001137.
15   Oliver, 'The Role of Traditional Medicine'.
16   Nakata, 'Pathways for Indigenous Education'.
17   Rose, 'Love in the Time of Extinctions', 83.
18   Roy Patterson, in conversation with Jennifer Jones, 15 April 2016, DS300142.
19   Bleakley, 'Animals and Information', 132.

Bunjil is the creator, Bunjil gave life to Mother Earth, to flora and fauna. Bunjil gave us bush tucker, bush medicine and our way of life. They are a beautiful animal and the creator that made us in our Dreamtime. That is why I am so proud of them.

When I go to the Healesville Sanctuary to watch the birds of prey, Bunjil comes up behind me and talks to me, especially one young female eagle. She will not shut up. She is a beautiful bird; I've got one of her feathers at home. The male eagle was shot by the farmer; the wildlife people had to go up and put him out of his misery. When I die, the feathers go to me grandchildren. The feathers carry Bunjil's spirit.

One bloke at the Healesville Sanctuary says to me, 'Uncle, this one Bunjil never stops watchin' you all the time you're with me'. I can rub me hand up and down her chest and she is lovin' it. He says, 'I've never seen her do that'. He said, 'why do you reckon that is Uncle?' I said, 'the spirit of the Aboriginal people'. He says, 'you are probably right'.[20]

Uncle Roy held deep sympathy for Bunjil and their suffering under the impact of colonisation. He observed the eagle's management of a changed diet, and the spiritual haven that both eagle and Aboriginal people find at Camp Jungai:

Whenever an eagle eats rabbit, dead sheep, dead cattle, whatever, the fur goes in down their throat and they get a fur ball. Every now and again they cough the fur ball up. They go down to a special tree at Camp Jungai down by the Rubicon River where they cough up. I do believe when they cough up their fur ball, they cough up part of their spirit and you can actually feel that spirit and the power of it down around those trees. I've had Elders come down from New South Wales and Queensland, and I've taken them down there, and they didn't know our culture or nothing, but they sat down on the ground there and they never moved. They spend the whole day there because they could feel the spirit. I feel it every time I go down there. In fact, I feel Bunjil every time I come up to Camp Jungai. This is a very spiritual place.[21]

---

20   Roy Patterson, in conversation with Jennifer Jones, 3 March 2016, DS3001139.
21   Roy Patterson, in conversation with Jennifer Jones, 29 April 2016, DS300148–53.

Camp Jungai is an ancestral ceremonial site that has been an outdoor education camp since the 1970s. It remains an important place of refuge, cultural maintenance and recuperation. Several of our bush tucker journeys started or ended at Camp Jungai, as important plant specimens are nurtured there by Taungurung people and camp employees. Providing non-Indigenous people with access to cultural education at Camp Jungai also enables custodians to foster respect:

> Respect for our culture, respect for bush tucker, bush medicine and the spirit world. The Dreaming starts at birth and when you start to walk around, you start to learn. It goes through your whole life. The children are always watchin', and this is how they learn.[22]

Below is Uncle Roy's account of Taungurung culture as he understood it. Uncle Roy wanted to record, preserve and promote this generational knowledge. He makes plain that access to foods and medicines, and their preparation and sharing was determined by customary law and made safe by generational supervision. Readers are advised to exercise caution and asked to show respect for Taungurung intellectual property when engaging with natural resources.

Blackwood wattle (*Acacia melanoxylon*)

> I'm going to give you some leaves and we will find some water, and you are going make soap. It is marvellous. What you do is take the leaves and make a ball out of it. Put your hands under water to wet them and then rub together hard and fast until the suds come. It has its own perfume and is your skin moisturiser and healing substance for dermatitis. Grab the leaves and rub them together in water and it will make soap. The leaves of the blackwood wattle or the inner bark of the blackwood wattle. All you do is put both your hands in the water with the leaves and pull them out and rub hard and fast and it will go frothy. If you rub long enough, it will take the dye out of the leaves and the soap will go free. You can smell the perfume in it and your hands are so soft, it is unreal; absolutely beautiful. The trouble is that they have all been cut down around here.

---

22   Roy Patterson, in conversation with Jennifer Jones, 3 March 2016, DS3001138.

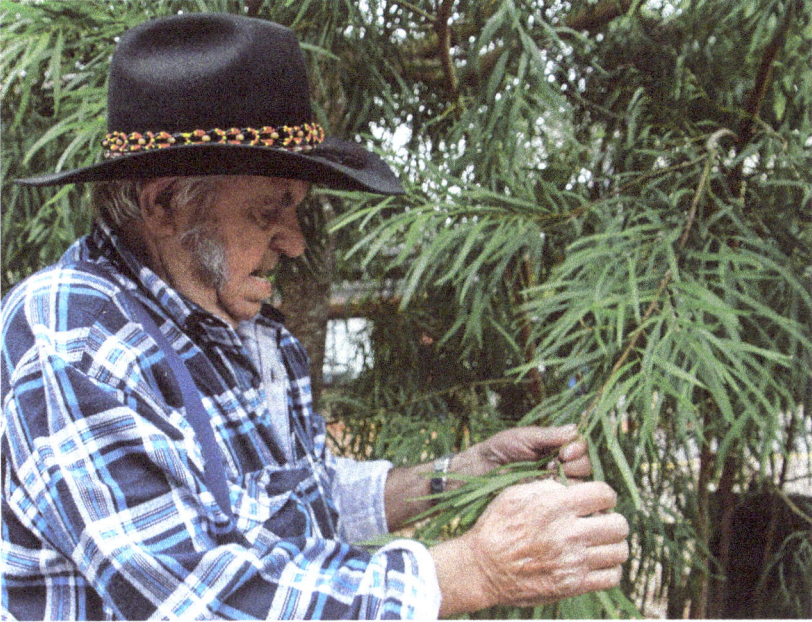

Blackwood wattle

Source: Photographed by Moorina Bonini.

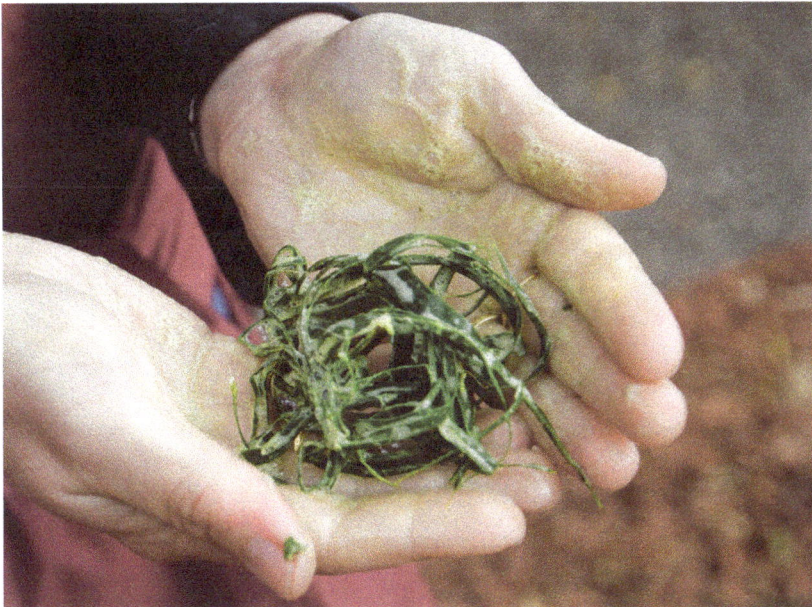

Blackwood wattle soap

Source: Photographed by Moorina Bonini.

Well, you can also take the seeds out of the seedpods and grind them down to make a flour. You can use it in damper, scones and cakes, or make a drink out of it and it tastes very similar to coffee. You can use the seed in ice cream or mix it with your food for extra flavouring.[23]

Bogong moths

Cathedral here has the Bogong moth, oh yeah, in the spring, September–October, the ground is *covered* with them! Up at Camp Jungai, the kids say, 'Uncle Roy, what are these things?' I say, 'They are moths, you can eat them!', 'Urgh!' they say. Aboriginal people cooked them. They put a small stick through the moth, hold it over the fire for a few minutes, then pull him out and eat him; tastes a little bit nutty. They used to cook 'em up and when they went walkabout they had them in a bag and ate 'em cold and kept on walkin'. They never went hungry.[24]

Bottle brush

With the bottle brush, you grab the plant between the thumb and forefinger, and lick the honey off the flower, or you put it in your mouth and suck it off. They got natural honey in them. Every time you see a bird or a bee going to a bottle brush, you can take the honey off it too.[25]

Bracken fern (*Pteridium esculentum*)

While the bracken fern is little on the end you can eat them; just pick them off. They are light and tender and have a nutty taste, beautiful.

These are food plants, but the bracken fern is also good for bull ant and jump jack bites as well; they are mean nasty ones when they sting ya! Just rub it straight on the sting and within seconds it goes away.

23 Roy Patterson, in conversation with Jennifer Jones, 15 April 2016, DS300143.
24 Roy Patterson, in conversation with Jennifer Jones, 8–9 November 2016, DS300158–66.
25 Roy Patterson, in conversation with Jennifer Jones, 29 May 2016, DS300148–53.

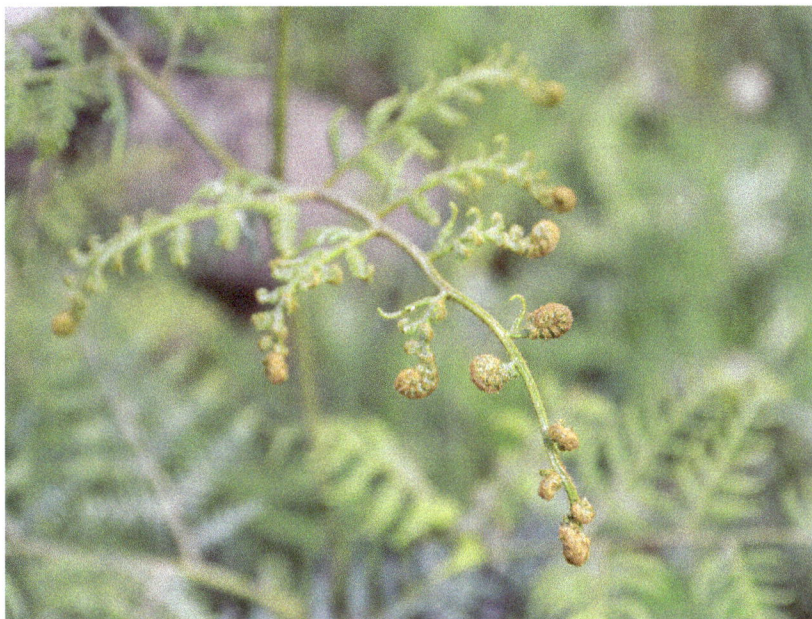

Bracken fern

Source: Photographed by Moorina Bonini.

My grandfather taught me about the bracken fern; put it in the water and wait for the fish to come to the top because it takes the oxygen out of the water and they come up to the top for the oxygen and 'bang, thank you' you've got them. You never took nothing that you didn't need.[26]

Burr

See this burr; if you get diarrhoea or gastro, you wash it and chew it and swallow the juice; chew and chew and chew until there is nothing left of the juice and then throw it out. Within 24 hours, your diarrhoea or gastro will be cured. Look how it grows here, I've got it everywhere at home in Taggerty.[27]

---

26 Roy Patterson, in conversation with Jennifer Jones, 12 July 2016, DS300154–56.
27 Roy Patterson, in conversation with Jennifer Jones, 8–9 November 2016, DS300158–66.

Burr

Source: Photographed by Moorina Bonini.

Buxton gum (*Eucalyptus crenulata*)

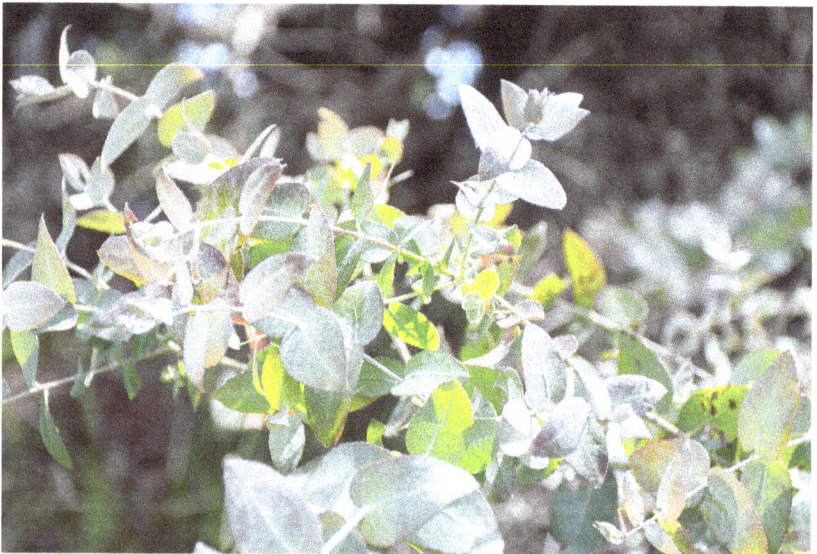

Buxton gum

Source: Photographed by Moorina Bonini.

The Buxton gum is a rare and endangered tree found on the alluvial flats of the Acheron River near Buxton. It is a distinctive small tree of irregular form, growing to 12 metres high. The bark of the mature tree is rough over most of the lower trunk, but smooth on the upper trunk and branches. The leaves are blue-green in colour and retain distinctive juvenile-type foliage throughout its life.[28] The leaf looks dry until you crush it, then it becomes shiny and sticky, releasing very strong fragrance:

> The daughter of a friend of mine had whooping cough, and when she got rid of that, she got a chest infection. So, I got some Aboriginal medicine called Buxton gum. The Buxton gum is only grown in this area, and it's a medicine that my ancestors used. Europeans have been destroying that tree for years. To use it naturally you grate it up, wrap it in material, warm the material up and wrap it around your neck; not too tight, so the warmth of the material goes into your neck and the vapour of the Buxton gum goes up into your nose and all the way down into your lungs. This young Indigenous fella said to me the other day, 'that goes right through the bloody house Uncle Roy!' I said, 'that's good, take some more leaf home, keep on doin' it. If you are runnin' short, come up and git some more. This will heal ya'. I said, 'keep it up a week or two and it will cure whatever infection you've got in your throat'. Grab a leaf, screw it up, put it to you nose and breathe in deep. This is where you get the original Vicks VapoRub from! But Vicks VapoRub ain't as good as the natural thing. In the summertime, it is an insect repellent. It is a natural medicine; we've been using it 50,000 years; you get a bit tight in the chest and you rub the leaves between your hands and breathe it in.

> Birds eat the seed and it won't dissolve in the bird's stomach. It comes out in the droppings and it grows stronger again and bigger and more beautiful. I've got this tree down at home, but it isn't as big as this one. I've been up here since 2002, and it was here then. The birds love it when the flowers come out, and so do the bees.

> Buxton gum is also a good bloody repellent; gets rid of flies. All eucalyptus is good. I've just made up a new mixture for me arthritis; eucalyptus oil, tea-tree oil and emu oil. Mix them together

---

28   Department of Sustainability and Environment, 'Buxton Gum', accessed 28 November 2017, www.environment.vic.gov.au/__data/assets/pdf_file/0022/32584/Buxton_Gum_Eucalyptus_crenulata.pdf.

and just rub it on and oh it is beautiful. So, we use everything we can. If you get a bit of a sprain, just get a eucalyptus leaf, twist it, break it and rub it on the sprain and what you are getting out of that leaf will start to ease the pain in that sprain.[29]

White correa (*Correa alba*)

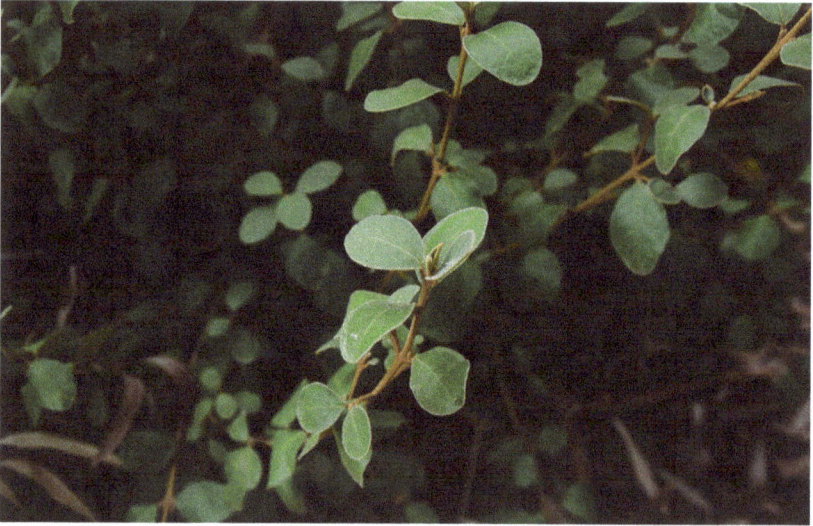

White correa

Source: Photographed by Moorina Bonini.

This is dense rounded shrub grows up to 1 metre in height and 2 metres in width. It has rounded grey-green leaves and bell-shaped white flowers:

> The 'correa' has a little round leaf. You grab the leaves and as it is cooking the flavour goes right through the meat, the same as garlic does, but it tastes like a cross between basil and a bay leaf. You will want to take this plant home! It is absolutely beautiful. When my ancestors killed a kangaroo or an emu, they took the stomach out and put these branches in where the stomach was and while the meat is cooking the flavour is going through the meat. Earlier in the year, we put it in barramundi; with green leaves in it where the stomach was, and I put it on the BBQ in paperbark. Yum! It is one of our very special herbs.[30]

---

29   Roy Patterson, in conversation with Jennifer Jones, 15 April 2016, DS300143.
30   Roy Patterson, in conversation with Jennifer Jones, 29 April 2016, DS300145–47.

Cumbungi or bullrush (*Typha latifolia*)

These are ones that are in the water and you go down and cut them off. You can eat the roots if you cook them.[31]

Dogwood tree grub

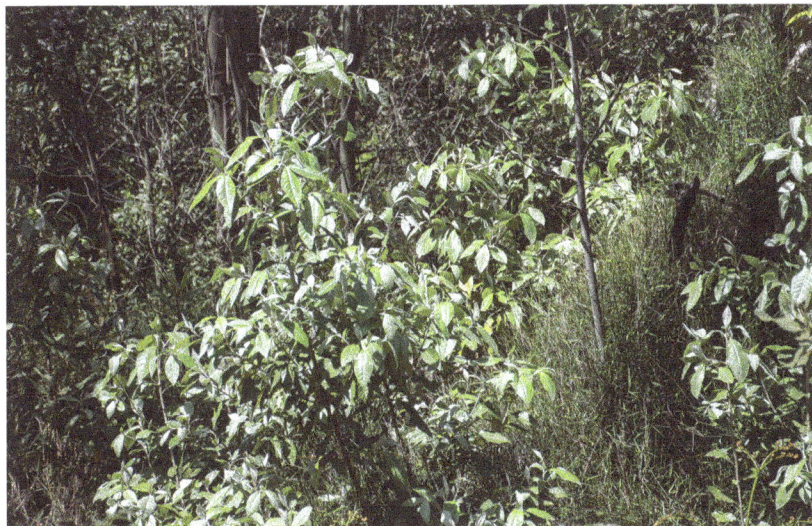

Dogwood tree
Source: Photographed by Moorina Bonini.

Non-Aboriginal attitudes to Australian edible grubs have been heavily influenced by culturally chauvinistic representations of Aboriginality. Edible grubs are larvae of moths that feed in the trunks of host plants. They provide a significant source of seasonal nutrition.[32]

The Dogwood grows beside mountain streams. The good thing about it is it gets a grub in it. When you look at the Dogwood, you see a little bit of sawdust where the grub has gone in. If it is a dark sawdust, it has been in there for a while. You break the spot open and the grub might be down further about 18 inches or 2 feet; grab it out and eat it. It tastes like peanut butter, I ain't jokin'. It happens in the spring, before all the moths come out. It only grows about

---

31 Roy Patterson, in conversation with Jennifer Jones, 29 April 2016, DS300148–53.
32 Yen et al., 'Current Issues'.

2 inches long and about the thickness of a match. They are an orangey colour. I tell you, they make good fish bait too, the fish love 'em, oh yeah, they are beautiful.[33]

Egg and bacon plant (*Eutaxia myrtifolia*)

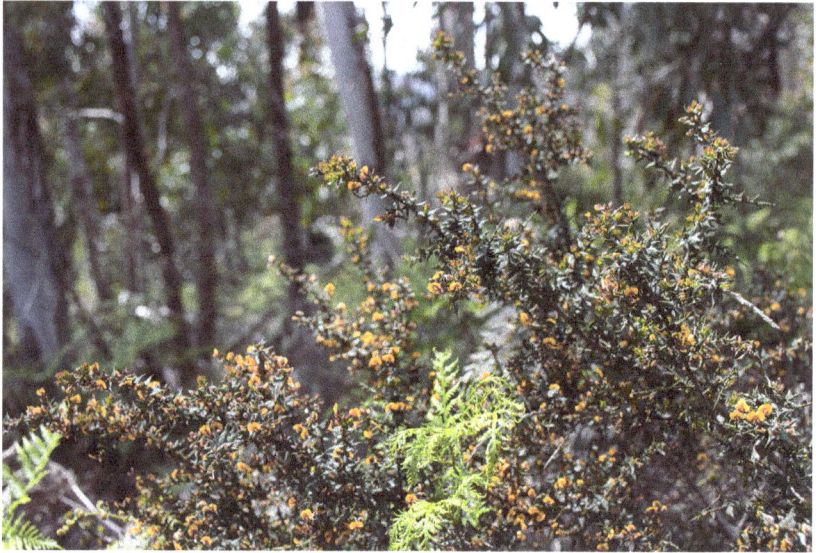

Egg and bacon plant
Source: Photographed by Moorina Bonini.

The egg and bacon plant; you boil up the flowers into a tea. You can drink it hot or cold and it's good for blood pressure: high or low. It's a medicine. It's a spring flowering plant. You put the branch and the leaves and all in, and it is already sweet.[34]

Fire as a bush management tool

We didn't burn the bush when it was bone dry. We burnt when there was dew on the ground; burn one section, then another section, then a section until they would burn into each other. We never let it get away from us.[35]

---

33 Roy Patterson, in conversation with Jennifer Jones, 8–9 November 2016, DS300158–66.
34 Roy Patterson, in conversation with Jennifer Jones, 8–9 November 2016, DS300158–66.
35 Roy Patterson, in conversation with Jennifer Jones, 12 July 2016, DS300154–56.

Fishing techniques

We used to use nets made out of grasses. Then we'd find a nice very slow pool flowing off fast water; put a rock around it to hold the net up and get bracken fern and take the dirt off the roots and crush it up. The white stuff that comes off the bracken fern, you put that into the water; any fish in there can't breathe because it takes the oxygen out of the water; and we can pick them up.[36]

Fish rib fern

Fish rib fern tastes like almond. This will do the same thing for ant bites and mosquito bites. It is powdery, so it makes your mouth dry as well. You only eat the young shoots as a snack, not the old ones. The ones with the curl on the end are the best one to eat; nice and fresh. They call it fish rib fern because the seeds look like fish eggs. Everything around here is educational; bush tucker and medicine and special sites.[37]

Fish rib fern
Source: Photographed by Moorina Bonini.

36 Roy Patterson, in conversation with Jennifer Jones, 12 July 2016, DS300154–56.
37 Roy Patterson, in conversation with Jennifer Jones, 29 April 2016, DS300145–47.

Kangaroo apple (*Solanum aviculare*)

Kangaroo apple
Source: Photographed by Moorina Bonini.

This tall shrub with glossy dark green leaves is found in higher rainfall areas. It has a delicate purple flower and edible fruit that starts green and turns yellow to orange and red as it ripens.

> The kangaroo apple plants here on Mount Cathedral has a purple flower that comes before the seed, when the perfume comes out. They are a relative of the deadly nightshade; one is black and the other is purple and they are deadly. But this is women's business, women's medicine, so I can't go any further.[38]

---

38   Roy Patterson, in conversation with Jennifer Jones, 8–9 November 2016, DS300158–66.

Lemon-scented tea-tree

Lemon-scented tea-tree

Source: Photographed by Moorina Bonini.

This beautiful plant here is the lemon-scented tea-tree. Rub that in your fingers and smell it. I've got one growing at home. When you are making a cuppa tea, put it in your tea and it makes beautiful herbal tea. The same with the young leaves of the eucalyptus tree. You pick 5 centimetres of the lemon-scented tea-tree and put it in your water with some native mint, and it stops motion sickness. You put it in the water, shake it up and get the flavours in the water and drink the water. I give it to the kids when they go home from Camp Jungai in the bus. When they get back to school the teachers thank me, because no one was sick on the bus! Otherwise, as they are going home they are spewing everywhere. I've got a son who even now cannot sit in the back seat, but he can sit in the back seat with a bottle with this stuff in it, and it will stop the squirmy tummy.[39]

---

39   Roy Patterson, in conversation with Jennifer Jones, 29 April 2016, DS300145–47.

Moss

Moss
Source: Photographed by Moorina Bonini.

Moss is the greatest antiseptic you can ever get for cuts and burns. If they've got a fresh cut or burn, you sit it moss-side down on the wound and, if you have a bandage, wrap it around. You can get some of that rib grass and wrap it around to hold it on.[40]

Mountain pepper (*Tasmannia lanceolata*)

Mountain pepper is a tall evergreen shrub or small tree of up to 10 metres high that prefers the cool wet habitats of high mountain gullies and the slopes of tall open forests. There are separate male and female plants. The trunk is straight, with distinctive reddish branchlets and leathery leaves that have an unusual fragrant, spicy flavour. Mountain pepper fruit is berry-like, about 5–8 millimetres in diameter, shiny, dark red, turning black when ripe. Initially they have aromatic, mildly spicy flavour, then, after a short delay, a more intense pepper taste.[41] Uncle Roy loved sharing his mountain pepper harvest:

40   Roy Patterson, in conversation with Jennifer Jones, 8–9 November 2016, DS300158–66.
41   Royal Botanic Gardens Victoria, '*Tasmannia lanceolata*, Mountain Pepper', accessed 24 April 2020, vicflora.rbg.vic.gov.au/flora/taxon/5505a156-251b-4f32-8711-f4e08c2ab9c2.

I can't get enough of mountain pepper. Every time I get it, I lose it, because people say, 'Oh, Uncle Roy, you got any more of that black pepper?' Two years ago, I got five ice cream containers full of those berries, and within a week I never had any left. My next-door neighbour, his daughter, daughter-in-law, staff at Camp Jungai and Holmesglen TAFE College—'Oh, I've got none left'. The leaf is just as good. It is very easy to pick, there are no thorns; they grow up in the Toolangi area. The native mountain pepper is a berry. You dry it out [in the oven] and grind it down and you've got a beautiful pepper. Get the leaf, and you can eat it raw; put it in a salad, put it in your stews or into your roast, and the flavour goes into the food. You bite and chew the leaf, and it is just like eatin' a little bird's-eye chilli, maybe not so hot, but it is warm! You pick the berry no later than the second week of March; they are also on the back of Mount Monda in the Narbethong Yarra Ranges National Park.[42]

Mountain pepper

Source: Photographed by Moorina Bonini.

---

42   Roy Patterson, in conversation with Jennifer Jones, 15 April 2016, DS300143.

Milk thistle

> If you have got a wart, break the milk thistle off and when the milk comes out, spread it over and let it dry and you'll get rid of the wart. They have a white flower when they open.

'Native Bread' (*Polyporus mylittae*)

The staple diets of Taungurung people were severely disrupted once land clearance and cultivation intensified in the Taggerty district. Marion Arminell Burchall was a four-year-old child when her parents selected densely timbered land for clearance and farming near Taggerty in 1876. In her memoir, she recalled that Aboriginal clans periodically returned to the Upper Goulburn River district from Coranderrk, camping near their family farm on their way to Thornton:

> We used to go over to the camps on our way home from school. When they camped they always built Mia Mia's. They used to dig up yams out of the ground to eat [and] native bread (a big white fungus). Sometimes my father used to find big lumps of native bread when he was ploughing and he used to make it into round balls for us to play with.[43]

Uncle Roy recalled:

> There was a yellow fungi that grows above ground and down below it in the ground the fungi grows in a big ball; up to 20 kilos. That used to be our bread; get a fire going, cook it and eat it. You couldn't eat it without being cooked. The fungi up top, the mushroom, it's got all the seeds, so you leave that there where you found it.[44]

---

43 'Some True Stories about the Aborigines of Victoria for Vivienne Hulley and Audrey Bevan, Read by Mrs Marion Popple of Wymarong', Aborigines of Australia—Miscellaneous Reminiscences, Royal Historical Society of Victoria, MS 22545, Box 118/11.
44 Roy Patterson, in conversation with Jennifer Jones, 12 July 2016, DS300154–56.

Native cherry (*Exocarpus cupressiformis*)

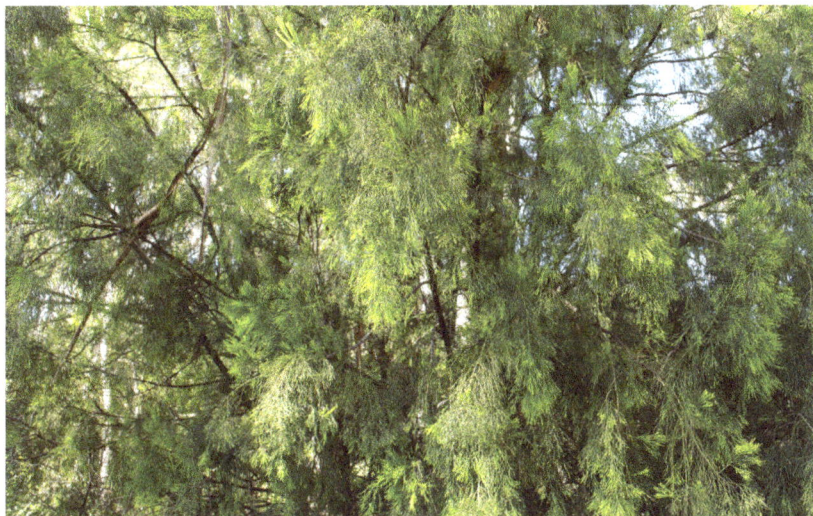

Native cherry
Source: Photographed by Moorina Bonini.

This small tree has the appearance of a conifer, with yellow-green weeping foliage and growing 3–8 metres high. Small cream flowers are followed by the fruit: a small, hard fruit supported on a larger, swollen and fleshy stalk that turns red, becoming sweet and palatable.[45] The wood from the native cherry was used for spearthrowers and bullroarers, and the sap for snakebite:

> The native cherry comes out in November too, but you've got to be quick to beat the birds to it. We used them for Christmas trees because of the red berry on them. They start off as a green berry about the size of your fingernail, then orange, then red; when they are red they are absolutely beautiful. They get about 1 centimetre or a bit bigger. The green part on the back is the seed; you eat the red part and throw the green part away. Awh, you won't leave them alone neither, once you start eatin' them. They going to be loaded this year, thanks to the good spring rain. I came up here to Camp Jungai one day with a group, and the tree was loaded. After the session, it was morning teatime and you couldn't see a student anywhere! They were all down there getting into the cherries![46]

45   Royal Botanic Gardens Victoria, '*Exocarpos cupressiformis*, Cherry Ballart', accessed 24 April 2020, vicflora.rbg.vic.gov.au/flora/taxon/10a16917-01e0-46cc-8bd8-359df2467806.
46   Roy Patterson, in conversation with Jennifer Jones, 29 April 2016, DS300148–53.

Native mint (*Mentha australis*)

Native mint
Source: Photographed by Moorina Bonini.

Pick a leaf off that and eat it. You can tell the difference between native mint and European mint because the stem of the native mint is square, while European mint is round. It only grows in this area, there are five different types. The ones here include:

- Natural peppermint: It isn't as strong as the mint. It has the same square stem but a softer taste.

- Native river mint: It is coming out of the ground here because it's been recently flooded. It had a purple edge as a young plant, when it first comes out, then it goes green. You can eat that now; it's strong and beautiful in a cup of tea. It grows about 50 centimetres high. They die off in the summertime and come back in the wintertime. This is the native mint to mix in with your water for motion sickness.[47]

---

47 Roy Patterson, in conversation with Jennifer Jones, 29 April 2016, DS300145–47.

Native raspberry (*Rubus parvifolius*)

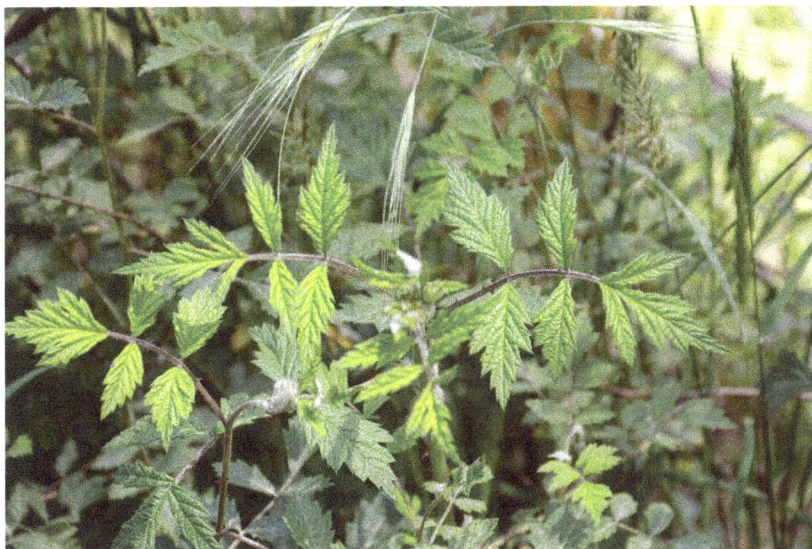

Native raspberry
Source: Photographed by Moorina Bonini.

This scrambling, prickly shrub or bramble has small bright green, wrinkled leaves and small, delicious fruit. Growing in mountain gullies, the native raspberry has often been displaced by the introduced blackberry, also a *Rubus* species:[48]

> The native raspberry: it looks a bit like a blackberry bush, but the leaves stay small. White people call them blackberries, but they have a smaller leaf and smaller berry and they are sweeter. The berries make better jam than blackberries. My mother, when we were kids, 'all you buggers, go and get me some raspberries'. We'd come back with a couple of bucketful's and mum would make native raspberry jam, ahh! It's better than blackberry and I *love* blackberry I can tell ya. But they spray them all with poison thinking that they are blackberries and kill them. They are very similar, they start off green, go red, and then black, but a smaller berry. They are beautiful.[49]

---

48   Royal Botanic Gardens Victoria, '*Rubus parvifolius*, Small Leaf Bramble', viewed 24 April 2020, vicflora.rbg.vic.gov.au/flora/taxon/bc19413d-6b07-4c94-84ee-4b5fef7e2f98.
49   Roy Patterson, in conversation with Jennifer Jones, 3 March 2016, DS3001139.

Orchids[50]

> With the orchid, you dig the bulbs out, but leave the flower there because the seed's in the flower. If you pick the flower and take it, you destroy the plant. There aren't many orchids around here now; I was down at Mitcham down near Nunawading, and this bloke was an expert on the orchid. He said that he used to come up here and get all the orchids. That is why they started to disappear. He didn't realise that he was taking the seed away. I wasn't very pleasant to him! I said to him, 'the big bulbs on the bottom; that's your tucker, not the seed'. Not only him, people would be driving along the road and would see a beautiful flower and say, 'we'll pick that', and they take the seed away. We lose a lot of our stuff because of that.[51]

Prickly currant (*Coprosma quadrifida*)

This prickly plant is an erect, open to dense shrub with fine spines on its branches. It has sweet edible red fruit from January to March:[52]

> The prickly currant is real bushy, just snip the dead branches off and let it grow in the winter. It starts off green and when it turns red, you can eat it, and eat it, and eat it! You won't stop eating it! The kids all know about it. Awh, they are beautiful eating. The fruit comes all along the stem here and they are absolutely gorgeous. Once you start, you can't stop. You just grab them and eat them. It is indigenous to here, all along the river you will see it. There is another prickly current, they are all along here. This is why we never went hungry. Can you blame us for going crook when white people took all our bush tucker away and our bush medicine? The majority of what you eat is also medicine.[53]

---

50 For a list of threatened orchids of the district, see Statewide Integrated Flora and Fauna Teams, 'Threatened Flora Yarra Ranges Shire', viewed 11 May 2020, www.swifft.net.au/cb_pages/threatened_flora_yarra_ranges_shire.php.

51 Roy Patterson, in conversation with Jennifer Jones, 12 July 2016, DS300154–56.

52 Royal Botanic Gardens Victoria, '*Coprosma quadrifida*, Prickly Currant', accessed 24 April 2020, vicflora.rbg.vic.gov.au/flora/taxon/1b8f3911-2ea5-499d-88af-ffe7fc4dbdb4.

53 Roy Patterson, in conversation with Jennifer Jones, 29 April 2016, DS300148–53.

Prickly currant

Source: Photographed by Moorina Bonini.

Rib grass

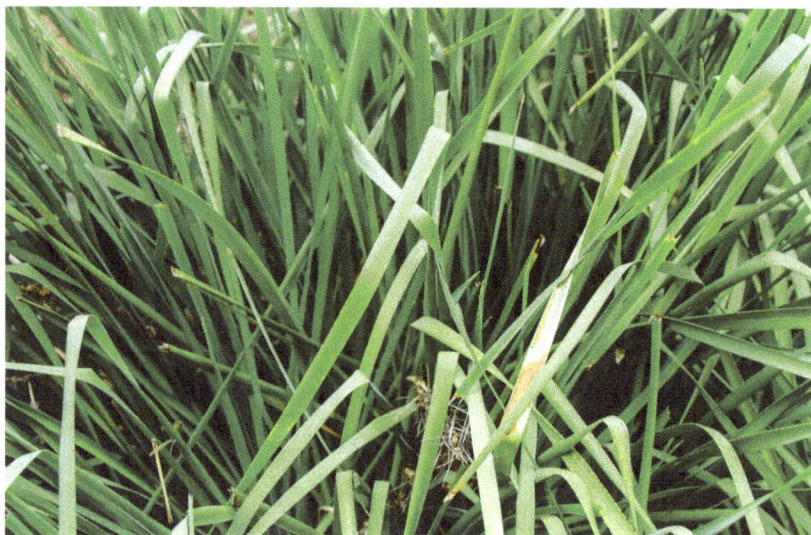

Rib grass
Source: Photographed by Moorina Bonini.

With this one, you eat the white bit; it tastes a bit like snow pea. You can grow this at home and put the white part in your salad. The white bit is the medicine. If you cut yourself or burn yourself, wind the rib grass around it tight, and two or three hours later you can take it off and you won't see where you have burnt yourself and the cut will heal from the inside out, not the outside in. A young bloke I know had a bad burn on his hand. He said, 'what am I going to do with this Uncle?' Got a few plants here, ribbon grass, cut the white part of it and stuck it on, put another one around it, and another one for about three hours. A young woman come to see what I was doing, and she had a big cut on her leg, 'what am I going to do with this Uncle?' Same thing, for two or three hours. After that, take it off and you couldn't even see the burn or the cut. They said, is this Blackfella medicine? I said 'yeah', and they couldn't thank me enough. I said, 'it's also tucker', and they said, 'what do you mean?', and I gave one to each one of them and said, 'eat the white bit and tell me what it tastes like', so they tasted it, 'it tastes like a snow pea'. They were right on the bloody knocker. It grows into a big bush, but up there they are rippin' it out, left, right and centre. People who don't know what they are doing try to get rid of them, but they still grow again, and it is beautiful.

Now with this one, when you twist it, it makes it stronger. Put the white bit in your mouth and then plait the strands. You can do weaving with these as well, basket weaving.[54]

River blackfish (*Gadopsis marmoratu*)

Up here, we've got 'slimies', which is a river blackfish; you go to pick them up and they slip out of your hand. We used to use nets, made out of grasses. Then we'd find a nice very slow pool flowing off fast water; put a rock around it to hold the net up, get bracken fern and take the dirt off the roots and crush it up. The white stuff that comes off the bracken fern, you put that into the water; any fish in there can't breathe because it takes the oxygen out of the water; and we can pick them up.[55]

River red gum

This is the flowering river red gum. These young eucalyptus leaves, take the bright green, small young tips off the end of it and put it in your tea, and you get a eucalyptus flavour and it is beautiful. Now, the flowers form nuts when the flowers drop off. Our ancestor women used to make necklaces and that out of them. Before that, they've got sweet nectar in them, natural pure honey. You ought to see the bees go for it: bush lollies, ooh yeah! You watch the birds and the bees get honey, and you can eat it.

This is only a very young tree; it will grow into a big one. Rub these leaves together in the palm of your hand and then smell them; strong eucalyptus opens up the airway into your lungs. It's absolutely beautiful. You smell it like that and it clears the airway right into your lungs.[56]

Early colonist Dr W.H. Baylie recorded the pleasure of watching Aboriginal mothers teaching their babies, barely yet able to crawl, to find the sweet sap of the gum. In 1843 he wrote: 'she provides [the infant] with a gum stick and teaches the little thing to search for exudation [gum or sap] upon it, which they esteem so as a great luxury in their repasts'.[57]

---

54   Roy Patterson, in conversation with Jennifer Jones, 3 March 2016, DS3001139.
55   Roy Patterson, in conversation with Jennifer Jones, 12 July 2016, DS300154–56.
56   Roy Patterson, in conversation with Jennifer Jones, 8–9 November 2016, DS300158–66.
57   Baylie, 'On the Aborigines of the Goulburn District', 135.

River red gum
Source: Photographed by Moorina Bonini.

Scar trees

See that scar on that river red gum, that is a coolamon scar. They took the bark for a coolamon, which is a carrying basket, but they didn't do it properly and the tree has grown bark back over to protect itself. It should have been on the shady side away from the north sun, then the bark wouldn't have to grow over the top. See this? This old scar: that is the shape of a canoe to go on the river. The bark was taken off this tree many, many years ago. There is another one down there. They were in the shade and protected, so it doesn't matter if it is on the north-east side, because it has got good shade. That one down there is a modern-day one. What you do is, you've got to cut around the shape that you want it. Then you get a stick, like a small sapling, you slowly put it in behind the bark, so you don't crack it and break it. It can take you 10–12 days to get that off the tree. You keep sliding the wood up and down it; what you are doing is breaking the sapwood and slowly lifting the bark off the wood. The bark is about 25–30 centimetres thick. They might have only used it to cross the river, and then come back again.[58]

---

58   Roy Patterson, in conversation with Jennifer Jones, 9 November 2016, DS300158–66.

Scar tree

Source: Photographed by Moorina Bonini.

Sword grass (*Lomandra longifolia*)

Sword grass
Source: Photographed by Moorina Bonini.

Sword grass—edible white flesh
Source: Photographed by Moorina Bonini.

This large perennial tussock grass has multiple uses:

> This is the sword grass. The edges are nasty; they will rip your hand right open quicker than a knife. I'm going to use a stick to wrap it around and pull until hopefully it will come out. You strip away the brown edges and the white flesh at the bottom you can eat. It tastes nutty, like macadamia nut. You can eat right to the green section.

> If you really look around here, there is food. This is also bush medicine; if you cut yourself and bind this onto the wound, it will heal. It is better than white people's medicine, because it heals from the inside out, not from the outside in. It congeals the blood and heals from the inside out; it doesn't leave a scar and doesn't need stitching.[59]

Tea-tree (*Leptospermum laevigatum*)

This tall, bushy shrub or small tree grows up to 6 metres tall. It has bark that sheds in strips:

> You can break the leaves off this tea-tree and make a drink out of it; hot or cold it is a medicine and the best thirst-quenching drink you can get.[60]

Tree fern (*Dicksonia antarctica*)

Tree ferns have an erect stem of up to 15 metres that forms a trunk, from which large green, roughly textured fronds spread, up to 6 metres in diameter. They grow in moist gullies and creek beds, and in high altitude forests:[61]

> The tree fern makes your mouth very dry, so to eat the tree fern, you take a little stone and roll it around your mouth, until it increases the saliva. The tree fern tastes like walnut. We keep these little stones all the time in our pocket. If you get bit by a big bull ant, rub this straight on and in seconds the sting goes away; and it works on mosquito bites.[62]

---

59   Roy Patterson, in conversation with Jennifer Jones, 8–9 November 2016, DS300158–66.
60   Roy Patterson, in conversation with Jennifer Jones, 29 April 2016, DS300148–53.
61   Australian National Botanic Gardens and Centre for Australian National Biodiversity Research, 'Tree Ferns', accessed 29 November 2017, www.anbg.gov.au/gnp/interns-2003/dicksonia-antarctica.html.
62   Roy Patterson, in conversation with Jennifer Jones, 29 April 2016, DS300148–53.

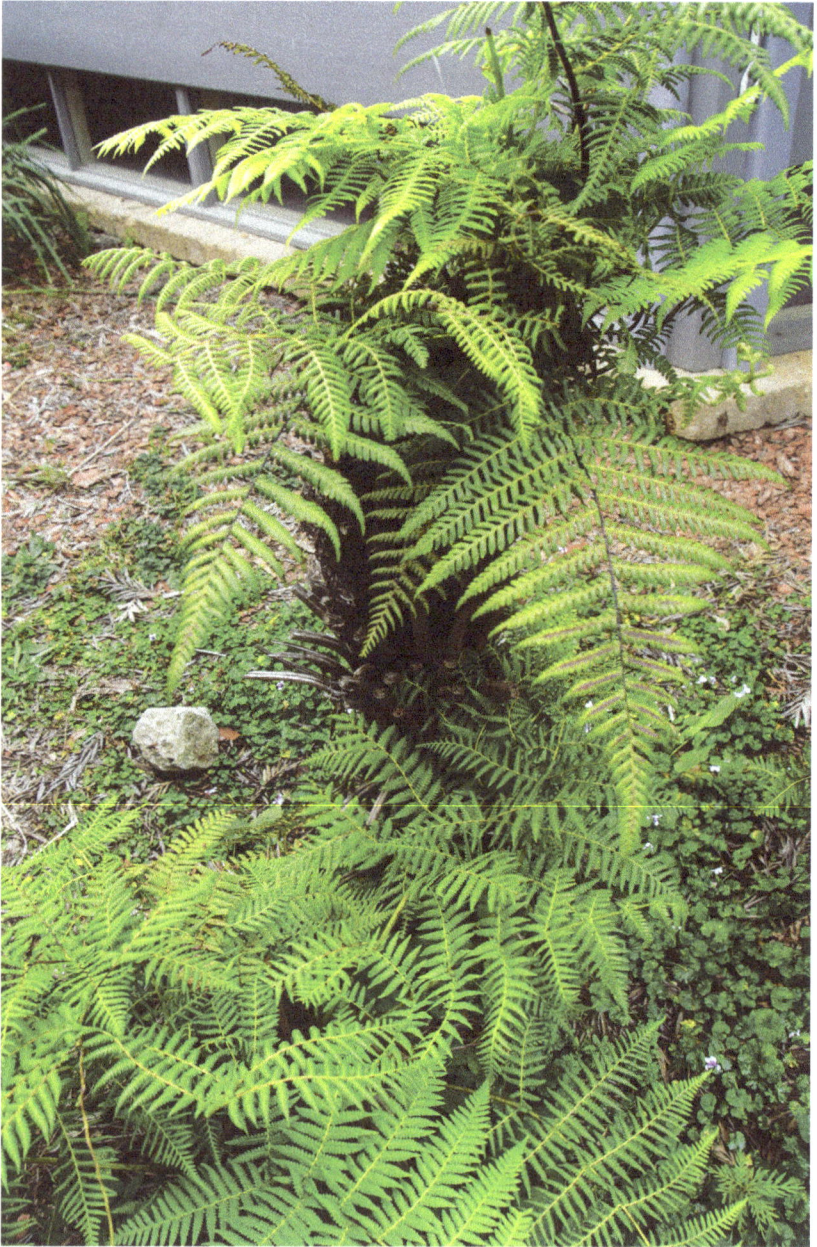

Tree fern
Source: Photographed by Moorina Bonini.

Warrigal greens (*Tetragonia tetragonioides*)

Also known as native spinach, this scrambling, leafy ground cover is high in antioxidants:

> These bigger leaves, you can't eat raw; you have to blanch them and then fry them in butter or oil. Eat that. The small leaf, you can eat it raw and you would swear that you are eatin' bloody cabbage or brussel sprouts. They are a winter plant that needs plenty of water and dies off in the summertime. You go along the beach in south-eastern Victoria and they are growing in the sand down there. Pull the plant out by the root, put it in the ground at your place, and they will grow. It is a winter plant. I was up at Camp Jungai a couple of weeks ago. I finally got in contact with the gardener up there. I said, 'you know that warrigal green over there?' 'Yeah.' I said, '*do not* cut it in the winter. It is a winter plant; it grows in the winter.' They said, 'yeah, but it grows into the other plants!' I said, 'well don't be bloody ignorant and don't grow other plants around it!'[63]

Uncle Roy's stories about bush tucker and bush medicine were designed to change settler attitudes and behaviour. Here he draws attention to the impact of mundane, everyday actions that fail to accommodate the natural features of the native plants. By attributing agency to the plant, and defending its interests, Uncle Roy draws attention to injustices that occur when the vital relationship between humans and plants is overlooked.

Uncle Roy's advocacy for Taungurung Country drew upon his authority as a knowledgeable and experienced Elder. One of our bush tucker excursions, which concluded at a natural spring called Saint Ronan's Well, illustrated this status. The Black Spur was deviated to Saint Ronan's Well when the road was rebuilt 'following a less precipitous route' during the Great Depression.[64] This permanent water resource marked a stopping point on a traditional walking track used by Aboriginal people. It later served settlers and their horses en route to the goldfields, and still provides fresh, cold water today.

63　Roy Patterson, in conversation with Jennifer Jones, 3 March 2016, DS3001139.
64　Symonds, *Healesville*, 107.

Tree fern at Saint Ronan's Well
Source: Photographed by Moorina Bonini.

When we pulled up, we found a young Aboriginal mother and her children exploring the pool. It was a breezy day and her son, perhaps five years old, finished his water play and clambered up the rocky hillside with striking independence. Flushed with his achievement and adjusting to the new and daring height, he declined to make his way down when his mother called. As the boy headed further up the incline, the mother gestured towards Uncle Roy and called out: 'You'd better ask the Old Uncle here if you can go further up that hill'. The child turned, diverted by this suggestion and asked, 'why?' She replied, 'because it is his Country!' Satisfied by this logic, the boy clambered down the slope and stood behind his mother's skirts. Uncle Roy nodded with satisfaction. It is his Country, and he knew it:

> My history, what I know of it, I can't teach it enough. I got to keep on doin it. The only time I stop is when I can't talk any more. I tell everybody, 'what you learn here today, you go away and teach it'. That is how I am getting my ancestry, my culture, bush tucker, bush medicine around the country. I put it down to this; knowledge cost ya nothing and it is not heavy to carry around.[65]

---

65   Roy Patterson, in conversation with Jennifer Jones, 15 April 2016, DS300143.

7

'Without culture, you've got nothing': Taungurung cultural heritage

Uncle Roy's knowledge of Taungurung bush tucker and bush medicine, shared in Chapter 6, makes tangible the legacy of generational connections to Country that his family have maintained despite dispossession. This knowledge speaks to deep family belonging in the Upper Goulburn and Upper Yarra River valleys. Uncle Roy's understanding of the distinctive character of Taungurung culture was also informed by a personal history of wide travel and connection with diverse Aboriginal people and cultures. Uncle Roy recalls the understanding gained through comparison and contrast:

> All my life I've lived in Healesville except for a couple of years when I worked with circuses on the circuit with Ashton's Circus and Wirth's Circus. I worked with the elephants and as an entertainer, being a clown, putting up the tents, pulling it down, getting it all ready for a show. It was a good life. I was workin' hard, but I got to like it, even though it was very hard. We went right up into Queensland, Dubbo, Mudgee, all over the place. I met a lot of other Aboriginals and got talkin' to them. I learnt a lot about Aboriginal cultures then.[1]

---

1   Roy Patterson, in conversation with Jennifer Jones, 15 April 2016, DS3001141.

Uncle Roy placed lifelong importance on his reputation as a hard worker. This labouring identity meant a lot to him in his old age:

> Here I am at 75 and I still cut me own wood. Even with this crook shoulder, I am still swinging a splitting axe. I can't just sit down and do nothing![2]

The Patterson family established a generational niche in the timber industry after legislative changes allowed them to return to the Healesville district from Cummeragunja. Here they earnt a family reputation as skilled and reliable timber getters. Uncle Roy's family and personal history demonstrates how Aboriginal people resisted assimilation, took pride in their Aboriginality, and passed on cultural knowledge to the next generation while negotiating legislative and cultural oppression. Previous chapters have shown how specific legislation introduced by the Victorian Government in the nineteenth century attempted to circumscribe and control most aspects of Aboriginal life, including employment, marriage and child rearing. The assimilationist agenda of this legislation, combined with the attitude and actions of the settler community, reinforced the assumption that Aboriginal people would only find acceptance in mainstream society if they relinquished their culture. Yet, the experience of the Patterson family shows that the need for labour in rural communities also provided niches where Aboriginal culture could quietly thrive, away from the conformist pressure of majority culture.[3] Semi-autonomous work, such as that available in the timber industry, provided everyday spaces where Aboriginal people could pursue their cultural priorities. When he was a younger man, Uncle Roy found another niche that accepted Aboriginal labour and provided opportunities to learn more about Aboriginal cultures across Australia. As Uncle Roy's brother wryly noted at his wake: one day the circus was in Healesville, and so was Roy, and the next day the circus had packed up and gone, and so had Roy!

'I did what my ancestors did, we roamed'

Uncle Roy's circus adventure is part of a long history of Aboriginal engagement in rural recreation and entertainment industries, both within their home areas and as itinerant workers. When bush carnivals and

---

2   Roy Patterson, in conversation with Jennifer Jones, 15 April 2016, DS3001140.
3   Hunter, 'Rough Riding', 93.

agricultural shows brought boxing tents and rodeo fixtures to town, they soon attracted the attention of local Aboriginal communities. Trips to the annual agricultural show feature in Aboriginal autobiographies because they offered an exciting break from routine and, sometimes, rare public validation of Aboriginal identity.

Author Ruth Heggarty, for example, recalled the anticipation of being 'let loose' at the Murgon show in south-east Queensland. From the vantage point of the mission truck, she saw 'lots of camp people walking in, or riding bikes or horses, or in sulkies' making their way to the showground gates. Contexualised by her regulated life in the girls' dormitory at Cherbourg Aboriginal Settlement, a new dress and pocket money to spend freely at the local show represented rare excitement.[4] Bill Simon also recalled waiting impatiently for the annual Kendall show on the mid-north coast of New South Wales, when 'enough bottle collection money meant we could go on rides, eat hotdogs and go to sideshow alley'. Later, as an inmate at the notorious Kinchela Aboriginal Boys Home, Bill would scan the fighters lined up in the boxing tent at the Kempsey show, hoping to see his father, who supplemented the family income by competing in boxing fixtures around the district.[5] Skilled local Aboriginal men like Bill Simon's father took the opportunity to exhibit their prowess in social contexts that otherwise diminished Aboriginal masculinity, while also competing for significant prize money. Bill recalled recognising his Uncle Jim Simon in the boxing tent line-up, and that seeing him 'standing there, looking proud and strong … in his silk boxing robe filled me with pride'.[6]

The permanent workforce of travelling shows was supplemented by local Aboriginal talent and their displays of expertise in rough riding, animal handling and entertainment bolstered Aboriginal prestige in rural communities. Richard Broome's research into tent boxing troupes reveals that itinerant Aboriginal boxers were 'popular among the local Aboriginal community', many of whom 'turned out to see them on the line-up board or claimed a connection to them'.[7] Wendy Holland and Mark Valentine St Leon suggested that travelling show communities employed Aboriginal people not only on the basis of talent, but also in solidarity, because show people were also marginalised by mainstream Australian society.[8]

---

4 Hegarty, *Is That You, Ruthie?*, 84.

5 Simon, Montgomerie and Tuscano, *Back on the Block*, 8, 48.

6 Simon, Montgomerie and Tuscano, *Back on the Block*, 48.

7 Broome, 'Theatres of Power', 12, 21.

8 St Leon, 'Celebrated at First', 64; Holland, 'Reimagining Aboriginality', 95.

According to Holland, 'the entertainment world was a fringe culture with its own rules and mores which were more liberal than those of the dominant settled society'.[9] Circus life gave Uncle Roy an unexpected opening for hard work, wide travel and a break from restrictions that seemed to chaff back in Healesville. He recalls his early adventures:

> I spent two years, 1961 and 1963, with Ashton's Circus as a tent hand, truck driver [and] as a clown. We went from Healesville right over to Norseman in Western Australia in 12 months, runnin' around to all different towns. Then I went back home and came back into the sawmill here at Healesville. They knew what I could do. There used to be 25 sawmills on Healesville; there was plenty of work in the timber game. I got sick of that again and went back to Wirth's Circus.[10]

One of the key benefits of the circus life, for Uncle Roy, was the opportunity it provided to connect with Aboriginal communities across Australia. In the circus, he learnt more about Aboriginal cultures:

> As soon as Aboriginal people come in, I'd have a yarn with them, talk about their culture, talk about my culture; our laws and Dreamtime is very similar, but our totems are different. You can have kangaroos, wallabies, wombats, koalas, snakes, lizards, platypus, birds. I met a hell of a lot of people travelling round for those two years. Then I spent three years up in Darwin; I got out of the cold! Then came back and nearly bloody froze![11]

These periods away from Healesville, which lasted 15 years, reinforced Uncle Roy's appreciation of his distinctive Taungurung culture and history. He associated this time with the purposeful seasonal travel of his ancestors, which he described as 'roaming':

> When I was workin' at Healesville, I was happy, but something made me go; I did what my ancestors did, we roamed. I roamed right around Australia three times and it took me 15 years. I worked as I went, but I always came back to Healesville. Then in

---

9   Holland, 'Reimagining Aboriginality', 95.
10   Roy Patterson, in conversation with Jennifer Jones, 3 March 2016, DS3001137.
11   Roy Patterson, in conversation with Jennifer Jones, 3 March 2016, DS3001137.

2002, I came up here to Taggerty, and I said, 'I am home'. I could feel the weight liftin' off me, 'I'm home'. Now I'm not moving off my ancestral Country, not to live anyway.[12]

Uncle Roy shares his generational knowledge of Taungurung culture below, revealing a way of life that responded to the distinct character of the central Victorian environment. Generational fidelity to Taungurung cultural laws ensured clan sustainability. This knowledge was of such importance to Uncle Roy that he reiterated key points two, three and four times in different discussions. In each re-telling, Uncle Roy offered more significant detail, a strategy that reflects an Aboriginal approach to education. Each of Uncle Roy's re-tellings drew attention to core Taungurung values, to the effects of dispossession, and to the opportunity now available for current and future generations to mitigate the impact of such disruptions.

Seasonal travel and dress

The movement of Aboriginal people across their lands was seasonal and predicated upon sustainable management of food sources, as well as meeting spiritual obligations and maintaining relationships with affiliated clans and bordering nations. Land management strategies that were 'unbroken for thousands of years before European settlement', resulted in the integration and interdependence of clan migrations and environmental cycles.[13] These strategies included short periods of occupation in each place, firestick farming and other sustainable practices. Uncle Roy highlighted other practical motivations behind the seasonal movement of Taungurung people, including clan location in more temperate areas of their Country according to the season:

> In the wintertime our mob used to move from the mountains closer to the Murray, but during the spring and summer they come back down here again to the mountain country. They used to dress in kangaroo hide and used the porcupine quill to stitch them together. The possum skin coat is better known, but it was ceremonial; they used kangaroo skin for everyday because kangaroo hide is bigger, and they are just as warm as the possum ones.[14]

12 Roy Patterson, in conversation with Jennifer Jones, 15 April 2016, DS3001141.
13 Kneebone, 'Interpreting Traditional Culture'.
14 Roy Patterson, in conversation with Jennifer Jones, 12 July 2016, DS300154–56.

Some European settlers misunderstood Aboriginal movement, characterising purposeful travel as aimless nomadic wandering, giving the term 'walkabout' pejorative connotations. William Blandowski, a naturalist who collected specimens and described the physical geography and geology of Taungurung land during excursions to central Victoria in 1854, was arguably more sympathetic.[15] When Blandowski observed clan movement patterns near Seymour and in the 'Black Ranges, on the upper Goulburn River', he described Taungurung people as 'few in number, of a peaceable disposition, and distinguished by a local language and characteristic habits'.[16] He also noted how:

> In the commencement of October the Goulburn River falls to its proper level, the winter rains having then subsided; and the multitudes of fish which appear in its waters attract hither the tribes inhabiting the surrounding districts. At that season too, they subsist upon eggs, which may then be obtained in abundance; and upon turtle and river mollusca.[17]

Seasonally motivated relocation made a rich diversity of food sources available to Taungurung clans. Traditional modes of dress also maximised the comfort of Aboriginal people in a land of climatic extremes. Yet, when early colonists recorded their observation of Taungurung adaptation to the central Victorian environment, the descriptions were sometimes disparaging in tone. John Cotton reflected upon Aboriginal dress in a letter to his brother in March 1844, expressing a derisive envy of Aboriginal freedoms. While deeming the Taungurung possum skin cloaks appropriate to the 'primitive forest of Australia', he also noted that his European garb was far less suited to the demands of the Victorian mountain environment:

> Most of the men, although short in stature, are remarkably well formed and their appearance enveloped in their opossum skin rugs, which are light and handsome coverings, is very picturesque and appropriate in the primitive forest of Australia. Many of the heads remind me of those which are so worthily admired in Raphael's pictures, although the features are certainly not so fine. The women, too, have generally fine moulded limbs, and with their opossum rugs, bags and buckets and long sticks are

---

15 Perhaps because his German nationality also positioned him as an outsider in colonial Australia.
16 Darragh identifies this journey as taking place in September 1854. Darragh, 'William Blandowski', 34; Blandowski, 'Personal Observations', 23.
17 Blandowski, 'Personal Observations', 23–24.

appropriate objects in the Australian landscape. I cannot think that the freedom which their limbs have in their loose robes and the facility with which they are cast off must be more congenial to human nature than the tailored cloth and vestments of Europeans. We can scarcely walk sometimes on the dry, slippery grass as the shoe can have no purchase, and when I go to bathe I often wish that I had merely a loose robe to cast off.[18]

Portrayals of Indigenous people written in the early colonial period reflect the cultural prejudices of the day and are often expressed in insensitive terms. Nevertheless, these observations provide valuable insight into Taungurung cultural heritage. Settler colonists justified their dispossession of Aboriginal people by characterising them as primitive people living in a primordial land. John Cotton held the (then common) view that he had 'reclaimed' his station in the Upper Goulburn 'from a wild, unprofitable state, and enabled it to yield fruit and grain for the general support of mankind'. He argued that, before he took possession:

It was a wilderness and useless to all the world. It is now brought into cultivation or covered with cattle and sheep, and hundreds of individuals are profitably employed in collecting or conveying away, preparing or manufacturing the produce.[19]

Judging Taungurung lifestyles as 'primitive' also asserted that a hierarchical distance existed between the cultures of European settlers and Traditional Owners. After more than 200 years of exploiting and ultimately degrading the land for profit, settler Australians are now beginning to understand that there is much to learn from sustainable Aboriginal ways of living. Thus, when Uncle Roy speaks of the clans enduring the cold and wet weather in caves near Yarck, the challenge is to abandon condescending images of 'cave dwellers' inherited from Western hierarchical thinking. Instead, try to imagine taking welcome respite from inclement weather in a significant cultural space. As Uncle Roy relates:

The clans used to keep out the cold and wind in caves up the back of Yaark. One cave looks right out over the valley; it's a beautiful view.[20]

---

18   John Cotton to William Cotton, March 1844, in Mackaness, *The Correspondence of John Cotton*, 45.
19   John Cotton to William Cotton, February 1847, in Mackaness, *The Correspondence of John Cotton*, 54.
20   Roy Patterson, in conversation with Jennifer Jones, 12 July 2016, DS300154–56.

Taungurung burial practices

Uncle Roy continues:

> There was a young woman buried up in that cave and the
> university mob heard about her and came up and took the body
> away. They estimate the body to be about 2,000 years old. We are
> still trying to get that body back to put it back in the cave and close
> the cave up. If someone died there they would bury them there,
> right where they were camped. The Elders, they were wrapped in
> paperbark and put up a tree. If they went into the ground, they
> were put in the same position they were in their mother's womb
> before they were born.[21]

An early detailed account of this type of burial practice can be found
in Dr William Henry Baylie's recollections of Taungurung people,
titled 'On the Aborigines of the Goulburn District', which was printed
in the *Port Phillip Magazine* in 1843. Baylie described Taungurung
preparation for burial as 'reducing the body to a small compass, making
it outwardly appear like a large ball'.[22] While Baylie's description assists in
understanding the mechanics of the burial process, it does not clarify why
it was important for Taungurung people to practise this distinct custom.
Uncle Roy explained:

> They were put in the same position they were in their mother's
> womb before they were born because we come from Mother Earth
> and go back to Mother Earth. This is the most powerful part of our
> Dreaming. The Dreaming comes into every part of our lives: our
> dancing and corroboree, when we go walkabout, our relationship
> with our totems.[23]

Other Taungurung cultural practices associated with death and mourning
were observed by early settlers, including Joseph Hawdon, who overlanded
cattle from Port Phillip to Adelaide in 1838. Hawdon encountered
a Taungurung man in mourning array, near the banks of the Goulburn
River. He described the old man, who was occupied catching a possum in
a hollow tree, as having 'his head plastered with a coat of white clay, which

---

21   Roy Patterson, in conversation with Jennifer Jones, 15 April 2016, DS300141–42.
22   Baylie, 'On the Aborigines of the Goulburn District', 136.
23   Roy Patterson, in conversation with Jennifer Jones, 15 April 2016, DS300141–42.

is the mode in which the tribes wear mourning for their dead'.[24] William Blandowski also commented on the material culture of Taungurung mourning during his excursion to Seymour in 1855. He noted that select trees associated with initiation ceremonies became memorials upon the death of the individual:

> Each of the dead trees represent a member of the extinguished clan. [If] the person to whom the tree is thus dedicated dies, the foot of it is stripped of its bark, and it is killed by the application of fire; thus becoming a monument of the deceased. Hence, we need no longer be surprised at so frequently finding groups of dead trees in healthy and verdant forests, and surrounded by luxuriant vegetation.[25]

Blandowski referred, in closing, to the population shocks experienced by Aboriginal clans following white settlement. Richard Broome has estimated that the pre-contact population of 10,000 Aboriginal people in Victoria was reduced by 80 per cent in just two decades due to disease and violence. Low birth rates 'caused by poor nutrition, venereal disease, loss of land, and loss of faith in the future' compounded this population disaster.[26]

Clan leadership

In these circumstances, the wisdom of clan leaders and the strength of kinship ties became all the more significant. As Uncle Roy observes:

> The Ngurungaeta was nominated by the tribe because of his knowledge, hunting skills and respect for the people and our law. You can become an Elder as you get older, with your knowledge of your bush tucker and bush medicine, your hunting skills, fighting skills and your treatment of your people. If you want to cause trouble, you've got no hope. If you insult a woman or girl children, you've got no hope; it's how you treat other people.[27]

---

24 Hawdon, *The Journal of a Journey*, 23 January 1838, 15.
25 Blandowski, 'Personal Observations', 23.
26 Broome, *Aboriginal Victorians*, 92.
27 Roy Patterson, in conversation with Jennifer Jones, 12 July 2016, DS300154–56.

The influence and respect attributed to the Ngurungaeta (clan head), by Aboriginal people and settlers alike, can also be gauged in early colonial records. Dr William Baylie was appointed medical officer at the Goulburn River Aboriginal Protectorate in 1841 and his descriptions of Aboriginal cultural practices are based upon this experience. He generalised Aboriginal people as becoming 'wretched' and 'degraded' in the early post-contact period, but also acknowledged that they were 'men of like passions with myself' whose 'impressions of right and wrong [and] acuteness of memory afforded to my mind sufficient proofs that they were rational and social beings'.[28] Baylie's positive impressions of Aboriginal capacity were informed by the respectful and fond relationship he developed with the Ngurungaeta of the Taungurung Nira Balug clan, a man called Yabbee (also known Billy Hamilton).[29] Baylie observed in 1843 that clan movements were 'ordered by' the Ngurungaeta, including attending regular assemblies where clans and affiliated nations gathered for business and pleasure.[30] According to Robert Kenny, clan heads had authority over the management of land and resources in their clan's territory. They used the principle of reciprocity to negotiate safe access to the land and resources of their allies.[31] William Baylie was impressed by Yabbee and the quality of leadership he exercised when he 'formed a council' to direct the Taungurung community. Yabbee's influence among the Taungurung clans and within the Kulin Nation was assessed by Baylie to be 'very great': 'he was always at the head of every debate, and no matter how trivial the circumstance he was always consulted and his advice generally taken'.[32] Baylie continued:

> Messengers are despatched to inform each other of the intended meeting, and when the grand division advances [and] assembles, the men in one band and the women and children in another; a consultation is now kept for some time; as to whether they shall receive the other tribes in a friendly or a hostile manner, and after this has been arranged the old men … advance into conversation with the heads of the other tribes.[33]

Matters negotiated between clans and nations included marriage arrangements, which ensured cultural continuity and genetic health within small populations.

28   Baylie, 'On the Aborigines of the Goulburn District', 86.
29   Baylie, 'On the Aborigines of the Goulburn District', 86.
30   Baylie, 'On the Aborigines of the Goulburn District', 90, 137.
31   Kenny, 'Tricks or Treats?', 38.4.
32   Baylie, 'On the Aborigines of the Goulburn District', 137.
33   Baylie, 'On the Aborigines of the Goulburn District', 137.

Marriage patterns and clan sustainability

Uncle Roy explained Taungurung marriage traditions with reference to the highly developed prescriptions on choice of partner and how these practices were maintained:

> If a woman had a daughter, the girl could not marry into that clan or into a tribal clan. The boy, he can travel around and go and see a woman from another tribe and bring them in. The girl was taken to another tribe and offered to a male over there so that there wouldn't be any deformity in the children.[34]

Blandowski had opportunity to observe and describe these Taungurung marriage practices during his 1854 travels to the Upper Goulburn:

> The young man who wishes to marry, has first to look out for a wife amongst the girls or lubras of some neighbouring tribe, and having fixed his choice, his next care is to obtain her consent. This being managed the happy-couple straightway elope, and remain together in the bush for two nights and one day in order to elude the pretended search of the tribe to whom the female belonged. This concludes the ceremony, and the young man then returns with his wife to his own tribe. He is, however, laid under this peculiar injunction, that he must not see his mother-in-law any more.[35]

Blandowski refers here to 'mother-in-law avoidance', a Taungurung cultural injunction associated with marriage that was little understood by Europeans. Deference and obligation informed this constrained mode of interaction, which was characterised by social distance.[36] While not an observer of this avoidance behaviour himself, Blandowski described the account of 'M. Grant, an eye-witness':

> A mother-in-law having been descried approaching, a number of lubras formed a circle around the young man, and he himself covered his face with his hands;—this, while it screened the old lady from his sight, served as a warning to her not to approach, as she must never be informed by a third party of the presence of her son-in-law.[37]

---

34 Roy Patterson, in conversation with Jennifer Jones, 15 April 2016, DS3001140.
35 Blandowski, 'Personal Observations', 24–25.
36 Merlan, 'The Mother-in-Law Taboo', 106.
37 Blandowski, 'Personal Observations', 24–25.

Part of the conventions of respectful behaviour practised by Taungurung people, mother-in-law avoidance required a man to refrain from going near, looking at, speaking to or even mentioning his mother-in-law's name. All relationships between clan members were constrained by protocols of proper demeanour that fostered good relations. Boys were therefore taught to exercise 'reserve and circumspection towards all females from whom, in accordance with marriage rules, they could expect to receive a wife'.[38] Fransesca Merlan suggested that specific cultural principles undergirded these formalised interactions between in-laws. Behaviours that were in daily use around an Aboriginal hearth also underpinned more infrequent encounters, such as trade between geographically distant communities. Both types of interaction were mutually understood, formalised social linkages based on obligation and reciprocity.

Another means of obtaining a wife and ensuring genetic diversity in the clan was 'bride capture', a practice that targeted women from non-allied nations or outside groups. This practice was also little understood in settler colonial society. Bride capture gained the salacious attention of Europeans as a form of 'courtship with a club', becoming an exemplar of the exotic sexual practices of 'primitive people' that entrenched racialised thinking and assumed the cultural subjugation of women.[39] Colonists frequently characterised Aboriginal wives as holding slave status, based upon their misunderstanding of Aboriginal attitudes to sexuality and the gendered division of knowledge and work within a clan.[40] Aboriginal women had significant autonomy and authority in the management of gendered economic and ritual activities, and these roles provided important freedoms and status.[41] Thus, when Uncle Roy describes bride capture, he does so in very pragmatic terms and links the practice to clan sustainability, not to gender inequality:

> You get raided by another tribe because the men from another tribe want fresh women in the tribe or they start to interbreed, and you can't interbreed in Aboriginal law because all your children must be born in good condition ... The men, when they go out after women, they go out without the women and children and the Elders; a few of the older warriors stay back, and the others go out.

---

38 Hiatt, *Arguments about Aborigines,* 151.
39 Konishi, *The Aboriginal Male,* 7; Conor, '"A Species of Rough Gallantry"'.
40 Watson, 'Aboriginal Women's Laws', 19.
41 Russell, 'Dirty Domestics', 21.

> If they get women from another tribe, they bring them all back; all the girls and boys and the boys grow up to help defend the clan. That way there is fresh blood coming into the clan with the girls, the boys and the women. That is how you make your clan and tribe bigger.[42]

The viability of infant life is also framed in pragmatic rather than emotive terms:

> If there was a deformity, the mother would get up and the child would stay where it was born; if you were not healthy you were not meant to be in the clan or the tribe. The child born deformed wouldn't have a chance of life and that was our law. All your children must be born in good condition. They can't be born deformed because you've got to be healthy to go out digging or hunting. It was pretty hard for the women. There was no option on it.[43]

W. H. Baylie observed these birth control practices in 1843, noting that:

> Women destroy many of their children at birth, and cause preternatural confinements ... the difficulty of rearing their offspring may be the cause of this melancholy practice, but it is generally adopted.[44]

European reports on the frequency and rationale of Aboriginal infanticide, like Bailey's above, were not necessarily based upon trustworthy information and did not refer to Aboriginal perspectives on the practice. Infanticide, which was a form of birth control also practised by poor European women, caused a moral panic among the upper and middle classes in nineteenth-century Australia. This resulted in social condemnation of poor white women who practised infanticide and an increasing number of legal convictions. Yet, these individual cases were not, as Liz Conor has argued, generalised as reflecting a barbaric 'white custom', which is how infanticide was framed in Aboriginal communities.[45] Reports of Aboriginal infanticide and other tropes of deficient 'primitive maternity', although perhaps based upon rumour and exaggeration as Conor suggested, were nevertheless used to explain Aboriginal population decline in preference to acknowledging the effects of colonisation and dispossession. William Baylie concluded his note on Taungurung birth

---

42 Roy Patterson, in conversation with Jennifer Jones, 15 April 2016, DS300144.
43 Roy Patterson, in conversation with Jennifer Jones, 15 April 2016, DS300144.
44 Baylie, 'On the Aborigines of the Goulburn District', 135.
45 Conor, *Skin Deep*, 81.

control and parenting with a positive observation: 'to the children whom they rear they become greatly attached'.[46] This attachment, as Uncle Roy explains below, reflects group-oriented cultural values that contrast with the individualistic values of European settlers. Decisions regarding child rearing therefore reflect the paramount needs of the collective.

Family and clan

> The family and the clan are important, so if any strangers come around the animals give warning. The dingo or a pet goanna, or a bird gets disturbed and they wake the man up and he knows that trouble is comin'. He will defend the clan with all his might and the whole clan will join in; 70 or 80 people in the clan, half of those will be women and children, and the rest will be men. When you got 30 or 40 blokes there, you got a big mob all with spears, boomerangs and nulla nullas. The man is the last in line as far as bein' important. It's not because he is useless (although most are!) but because if any strangers are comin' in they have to get past him to get to the family.[47]

According to Uncle Roy, the kinship ties within the clan undergird Taungurung collective belonging:

> We live for each other, we protect each other; when you make a humpy in a camp; the children are up against the back of the wall, then the women, then the animals, then the man outside. He's got fires around him and a dog and he is up and ready to fight at any warning. It is a good way of life. There was no animosity in our law and our culture: very simple. The first and fundamental thing is respect. We haven't got it today because of the alcohol and drugs.[48]

The harmony of this social organisation, as Uncle Roy explains, has been undermined by the legacies of colonialism now manifest in Aboriginal lives. According to Indigenous scholar Irene Watson, Aboriginal people continue to struggle 'against the oppression of colonialism and for the sustainability of the collective'.[49] She has argued that policy that addresses

---

46 Baylie, 'On the Aborigines of the Goulburn District', 135.
47 Roy Patterson, in conversation with Jennifer Jones, 15 April 2016, DS300144.
48 Roy Patterson, in conversation with Jennifer Jones, 12 July 2016, DS300154–56.
49 Watson, 'Aboriginal Women's Laws', 26.

Indigenous experience, including the experience of violence, must acknowledge this prioritisation of collective belonging. Working for community benefit and prioritising respect for Elders ensures community cohesion. Uncle Roy continues:

> When they bring the food out, the best of the meat goes to the Elders who can't go hunting, both men and women; then the children; then the men and women get their food and that way everybody gets a feed. No one is left out. The ones that [hunt and gather] make sure that the best goes to the Elders who can't go out [anymore], which is a great thing.[50]

Aboriginal lifeways promote the sustainability of both the clan and their environment by prioritising harmonious relationships among individuals and community members. Irene Watson has argued that the Australian public still knows very little about Aboriginal law, which is 'a balance of women's, country and men's law'.[51] These three realms of law relate to 'the obligation to care for country and family, ecological sustainability, and the ethics of sharing and caring and their deeper philosophy'.[52]

Gendered knowledge and learning

Aboriginal cultural knowledge is managed and taught in complex gradations, ranging from open knowledge that is available to everyone, through to secret knowledge that is restricted according gender and authority.[53] When Uncle Roy describes Taungurung knowledge systems, he connects it explicitly to gendered instruction:

> There are two lores: men's lore and women's lore. When a woman has a boy child, she has him until he is about three years old and then she hands him over to the Elder so that the Elder can train him in tracking, hunting, weapon making and all men's business. The woman keeps the girls and teaches them. Men aren't allowed to go anywhere near women's business like the birth of a child and all that.[54]

---

50 Roy Patterson, in conversation with Jennifer Jones, 3 March 2016, DS3001138.
51 Watson, 'Aboriginal Women's Laws', 21.
52 Watson, 'Aboriginal Women's Laws', 20.
53 Rose, 'Women and Land Claims', 92.
54 Roy Patterson, in conversation with Jennifer Jones, 3 March 2016, DS3001138.

Gender and place-based learning are central to Aboriginal pedagogies, as teachers draw upon profound ancestral and personal connections to Country to contextualise learning objectives. Other key characteristics of Aboriginal pedagogy, according to Tyson Yankaporta, include group-oriented storytelling and modelling. This experiential approach to learning engages the student in repeated observation, listening and practice to gradually attain mastery.[55] William Baylie described this competency-based approach when he watched Aboriginal mothers teach their babies to swim in 1843:

> The children soon acquire the art of swimming; in the warm weather the mother takes her baby on her back and plunges into the water, the little thing soon gets accustomed to it, and at the age of five or six becomes a very good swimmer.[56]

Uncle Roy explains that the relationship between Elders and children is especially important. This is because the independent competence and mastery of the student is dependent upon the prowess of the Elder:

> The only time the mother has got anything to do with the boy is of an evening time and dinner. The rest of the time the Elders who are too old to go out and hunt have got him; they teach him weapons, artefacts, how to hunt and how to track, how to do anything a man does. Men also know the bush tucker and bush medicine; when he goes out he has to be able to gather all that food for himself because he doesn't take a woman with him. When they go out for the hunt, they remember what their Elders taught them.[57]

Recalling and enacting the knowledge handed down by the Elders and returning the benefit of this action to the community is central to Aboriginal pedagogy.[58] Another important characteristic of an Aboriginal approach to learning is the use of all the senses to engage students and to foster comprehension of deeper symbolic meanings. Performance, such as in a 'corroboree' or ritual practice, is therefore a significant strategy in Aboriginal education. As Maryrose Casey has explained: 'The layers of meaning within the performances were learned progressively through

---

55 Yunkaporta, 'Aboriginal Pedagogies', 45.
56 Baylie, 'On the Aborigines of the Goulburn District', 135.
57 Roy Patterson, in conversation with Jennifer Jones, 15 April 2016, DS300142.
58 Yunkaporta, 'Aboriginal Pedagogies', 48.

exposure to the words and movements and when the right questions were asked and answered'.[59] Performances are offered without explanation, requiring students to actively engage with what they have seen and heard. When they are ready to deepen their learning, the student is provided with appropriate information, therefore increasing their understanding. Ritual performances were a feature of daily life prior to European settlement. They fulfilled ceremonial obligations, enabled teaching and learning exchanges and provided entertainment. Such performances 'combined dance, song, mime, dialogue, musical accompaniment, body decorations and costume, set and props as well as the use of lighting from fire and moonlight'.[60] Uncle Roy explains:

> Women and men dance together after a hunt. The men bring the kangaroo or the wallabies or the emus home. The women— I've got respect for all of them, they work just as hard as a man, gathering bulbs and roots, goanna, porcupine, small wombats. The women do the dance of the gathering while the meat is cooking. Then the men do the dance of the hunt. The children are sittin' there watchin' and this is how they learn. Then, you've got the girls over there on one side, the boys over there on the other side. They never sit together.[61]

Based on his experience with Taungurung people on the Goulburn River Aboriginal Protectorate in the early 1840s, Dr William Baylie recalled how Aboriginal infants participated in cultural events. He noted:

> At an early age they are taught their principal amusement, the corroberry [sic], and it is amusing to see the pleasure the mother evinces at the sight of her infant with its little legs in motion, attempting to dance, when scarcely able to crawl about.[62]

Audience restrictions were enforced for Aboriginal performances that had ritual or teaching intentions. As Maryrose Casey has observed, intra- and inter-community gatherings included choreographed performances of ritual that fulfilled judicial and diplomatic functions, including the arrangement of marriage alliances.[63]

---

59 Casey, 'Colonists, Settlers', 63.
60 Casey, 'Colonists, Settlers', 56.
61 Roy Patterson, in conversation with Jennifer Jones, 3 March 2016, DS3001138.
62 Baylie, 'On the Aborigines of the Goulburn District', 135.
63 Casey, 'Performances of Belonging', 189.

Aboriginal people also initiated ritual performances as part of cross-cultural exchanges. These events provided opportunity to assert Aboriginal sovereignty and to educate settler audiences about Aboriginal culture. Even when the audience was wholly composed of Europeans, however, ceremonies were never translated or explained. This choice reflects the offer of Aboriginal knowledge to the settler on Aboriginal terms. The settler was required to engage with Aboriginal language and cultural values if they wanted to develop their understanding.[64] The Upper Goulburn squatter John Cotton noted such a performance during the gathering of two Taungurung clans near his station, Doogallook, on the Goulburn River near Yea in March 1844. It could be argued that Cotton's cultural competency was not significantly improved by his experience, as he remained unaware of the reason for the co-location of the clans and the performance of the ritual. He and his family took the opportunity to trade food (including cabbages, carrots and melons) and tobacco in exchange for possum skins and spears. In a letter to his brother, Cotton then described being admitted to a Taungurung ritual that was 'performed in the rudest manner imaginable':[65]

> The lubras or women and children are seated in a dense circle and beat second time with their right hands on their folded opossum skins, which sounds something like a muffled drum, for they all strike together with great precision. A singer, one of the men stands by the musicians beating time with two sticks, which if well selected give out a sound something approaching that of a triangle. A large fire is lighted before the performers, who presently issue from behind a tree or other shelter, one or two at a time, assume a position like a spread eagle, and shake their knees with rapid motion, beating time with two sticks. Their bodies are painted with pipe clay, and their ankles and feet enveloped in bands of leafy twigs; a girdle is around the waist. They shuffle about from place to place, exhibit their spread eagle performance, and after a time all collect together behind the singer, increasing the time of the beat until they finish with one loud, simultaneous beat and retire precipitately. Their movements are varied occasionally; sometimes they finish their act … with a loud scream and retire with quick motion; at others the beats are varied and they retire with slow movement. I was amused with this exhibition for two hours one night. It is not commenced until sometime after sunset.

---

64   Casey, 'Performances of Belonging', 193.
65   John Cotton to William Cotton, March 1844, in Mackaness, *The Correspondence of John Cotton*, 44.

> At the conclusion of the performance some of them came up to me and asked me for tobacco, which I promised to give them the next morning.[66]

Taungurung requests for tobacco after the performance indicate that the clan considered John Cotton's participation as an extension of a mutual relationship of exchange and obligation. Bartering cabbages for artefacts may have been of little consequence to Cotton, but from a Taungurung perspective, the exchange established or extended a relationship between the settler and the clan that was bound by protocols of 'right behaviour' (i.e. their expectations of proper conduct). Richard Broome has argued that Aboriginal people 'tried to impose their ideas of right behaviour on strangers in colonial times', even after they had been forced into unequal patron–client relationships.[67] Taungurung leaders believed that usurpation of their lands required recompense, and that John Cotton was therefore obliged to ensure access to their lands and to provide tobacco when they requested it. Taungurung expectation of right behaviour, expressed in the form of maintenance payments, persisted regardless of settler recalcitrance. Indeed, Taungurung insistence that settlers respect their culture and practise right behaviour was maintained despite evidence of systematic non-compliance.

Conclusion: Seeing Taungurung people on their own terms

Recalling his first sighting of Europeans as they crossed the Goulburn River at Mitchellstown in 1836, Yabbee, the Ngurungaeta of the Nira Balug clan, told Assistant Protector James Dredge of 'the dismay he and other blacks experienced when they first saw [the] white men [in] Major Mitchell's party' on their return journey north-east.[68] Fox and Phipps noted that Yabbee, who was apparently swimming in the Goulburn River at the time of Mitchell's crossing, was not observed by the Europeans. They argued, further, that Yabbee and his Taungurung clan members were philosophically unobservable because, 'in a European schema it [was] not necessary to know anything of Yabbee's existence before the arrival of Europeans with guns,

---

66   John Cotton to William Cotton, March 1844, in Mackaness, *The Correspondence of John Cotton*, 44–45.
67   Broome, 'There Were Vegetables', 43.3.
68   James Dredge, journal entry, 30 January 1840, quoted in Clark, *Goulburn River Aboriginal Protectorate*, 19.

boat and sextant'.[69] As this book has shown, European settlers would take more than 150 years to begin to comprehend their need to 'see' Aboriginal people on Aboriginal terms. Yabbee and his compatriots, by contrast, likely understood what the arrival of Europeans represented for Taungurung people long before any direct or personal encounters.

When Hume and Hovell's party of explorers paused on Taungurung land at the Broken River near Mansfield in 1824 (12 years prior to Mitchell's journey), they observed that the bark of a tree had been recently removed using a steel tomahawk.[70] Possession and use of such technology indicates that Taungurung people had been exposed to European goods, and to stories about the society that introduced such implements, in the years prior to the arrival of explorers and settlers.[71] Aboriginal trade routes facilitated the movement of goods between distant Aboriginal clans, and they also enabled the exchange of news and ideas. Aboriginal message systems were highly effective means of communicating across language barriers, to the extent that the 'first contact' between Europeans and Aboriginal people south of the Murray River, in 1824, probably eventuated years after these nations had first heard about the expanding European settlements to the north and south. Even with no direct experience of European settlers themselves, according to Robert Kenny, 'the Kulin people of Port Phillip would have known something of this expansion and its dire consequences'.[72] Thus, when Taungurung leaders established relationships with pastoralists, they did so strategically, to extract gains and to assert their sovereignty. Yabbee, for example, visited John Cotton at Doogallook Station whenever he 'was in the neighbourhood'.[73] Yabbee continued to visit despite being assessed and described patronisingly by Cotton as a 'half civilised black'. He was unsettling Cotton and maintaining relationship to traditional lands.[74]

Nearly 40 years later, Ngurungaeta of the Yeeun-illam-balluk clan, Thomas Bamfield, still expected Europeans to modify their behaviour to accommodate Aboriginal sovereignty, despite the closure of Acheron

---

69   Fox and Phipps, *Sweet Damper*, 15.
70   Parris, 'Early Mitchellstown', 128.
71   Kenny, 'Tricks or Treats?', 38.6.
72   Kenny, 'Tricks or Treats?', 38.7.
73   John Cotton to Marian Cotton, December 1846, in Mackaness, *The Correspondence of John Cotton*, 48.
74   John Cotton to Marian Cotton, December 1846, in Mackaness, *The Correspondence of John Cotton*, 48.

and Mohican stations and his experience of conflict with authorities over the management of Coranderrk Station. In his 1881 letter to the board appointed to enquire into the management of the Coranderrk Aboriginal Station, Bamfield testified: 'I think they [settlers] have done enough to this country to ruin the natives without taking it from us any more'.[75] As Richard Broome observed, Bamfield submitted his testimony because he saw a political opportunity to draw attention to 'the failure to extend right behaviour to "a poor black"'.[76] Taungurung objectives to educate and alter non-Aboriginal behaviour have remained constant since Yabbee and Thomas Bamfield led the clans. Uncle Roy wanted to see non-Aboriginal people modify their beliefs and lifestyles to show greater consideration and respect for Country. Caring for Country, as Sean Kerins has explained, 'encompasses being spiritually bound to Country through intimate connections with ancestral beings still present in the land and waters'.[77] Uncle Roy believed that the social fabric of the Taungurung community would be strengthened by revitalising connections to Country and by sharing cultural, spiritual and ecological knowledge. Feelings for ancestral Country prompted Uncle Roy to undertake a return migration up the Black Spur to his traditional lands. His mission in the final years of his life was to re-establish connections to Country through the preservation of place-dependent knowledge of bush tucker and bush medicine that, in his view, was endangered by forestry practices and lack of respect for Taungurung culture:

> Our Dreaming is our law, which includes respect for our culture, our bush tucker, our bush medicine and the spirit world. The Dreaming starts at birth and when you start to walk around and start to learn. It goes through your whole life. There has got to be more of it in the community so we can all get together and really do it.[78]

Uncle Roy also envisaged a wider movement of cultural revival based on Taungurung educational practices. He believed that Taungurung cultural ways could be recovered and strengthened. He wanted this book to instil wider respect for Taungurung clan values—a measure of the 'little bit' that he could do.

---

75 Thomas Bamfield [alias Tommy Michie, alias 'Punch'], letter tabled 30 September 1881, in Victoria, Parliament, *Report of the Board*, 8.
76 Broome, 'There Were Vegetables', 43.11.
77 Kerins, 'Caring for Country', 29.
78 Roy Patterson, in conversation with Jennifer Jones, 15 April 2016, DS300141–42.

8

Conclusion

Should I have been surprised on the morning of Uncle Roy's funeral to see a police car at Eildon cemetery? Perhaps this was a funeral escort, I thought, a fitting gesture for a respected local Elder. But the hearse was already at the graveside, and the funeral director seemed surprised to see the marked police car. This was no escort. Parked conspicuously in the only entrance, the officers appeared to be issuing defect notices to mourners.

This was an Aboriginal funeral, and the 'old enemy' was on the offensive. As relatives ran the blue gauntlet, Uncle Roy's daughter sighed: 'I hope it's not going to be one of "those" days', she said, with a shrug of resignation. I can understand why Aboriginal people might become bitter in such circumstances. Uncle Roy would have laughed and said, 'would ya blame me?'

Yet, in his final years, Uncle Roy was committed to collaboration and made efforts to overcome past failings. He wanted solutions for Aboriginal people and healing for Taungurung land. Uncle Roy took his role as an Indigenous educator seriously; even his burial was instructive. He chose a natural burial, with a shroud instead of a casket so that his body would soon be held by Mother Earth. There was no fake green grass to soften the grave side, no polished brass, no piped music, no canopy to shade the mourners, and no white plastic seats in a neat line. We stood in messy huddles around the naked hole. The eucalyptus smoke and the stark, haunting sound of the digeridoo swirled around us as birds called. A grandson laughed out loud as he read surprising details in the eulogy. People shared anecdotes about an old joker, a teacher, a friend. Uncle Roy's body was lowered all the way to the bottom of the grave. His little great-granddaughter wailed inconsolably, clinging to her grandmother's trouser leg. Mourners threw gum leaves and ochre onto Uncle Roy's old Akubra, placed over his heart. I had never seen him without that old hat. I would never see either again.

Uncle Roy once said, 'here is a story for ya':

> In our Dreaming, the start of Aboriginal people is from Mother Earth. No one owns Mother Earth, not the state or federal government, not the mining companies and not the Aboriginals. When Mother Earth made people, she made us custodians of the land, not the owner. You don't own your mother, you are part of her; you belong to her. That's our law and a bit of our culture and spirit world. How do you like that?[1]

---

1   Roy Patterson, in conversation with Jennifer Jones, 3 March 2016, DS3001138.

Bibliography

Archives

Mitchell Library, State Library of New South Wales. William Thomas Papers, 1834–1868, MSS 214/19.

National Archives of Australia. B312, 1–5; B314, Roll 1; B335/0.

Public Record Office Victoria. Probate and Administration Files, VPRS 28.

Royal Historical Society of Victoria. Aborigines of Australia—Miscellaneous Reminiscences, MS 22545.

State Library of Victoria. Correspondence with Ngaire von Sturmer, MS 12242.

Government reports

Victoria. *Report of the Commissioners Appointed to Inquire into the Present Condition of the Aborigines of This Colony, and to Advise as to the Best Means of Caring for, and Dealing with Them, in the Future: Together with Minutes of Evidence and Appendices.* Melbourne: John Ferres, Government Printer, 1877.

Victoria. Parliament. *First Report of Central Board Appointed to Watch Over the Interests of the Aborigines in the Colony.* Melbourne: John Ferres, Government Printer, 1861.

Victoria. Parliament. *Fourth Report of the Central Board Appointed to Watch Over the Interests of the Aborigines in the Colony of Victoria.* Melbourne: John Ferres, Government Printer, 1864.

Victoria. Parliament. *Report of the Board Appointed to Enquire into, and Report upon, the Present Condition and Management of the Coranderrk Aboriginal Station, Together with the Minutes of Evidence.* Melbourne: John Ferres, Government Printer, 1882.

Victoria. Parliament. *Report of the Select Committee of the Legislative Council on the Aborigines*. Melbourne: Government Printer, 1859.

Victoria. Parliament. *Second Report of the Central Board Appointed to Watch Over the Interests of the Aborigines in the Colony of Victoria*. Melbourne: John Ferres, Government Printer, 1862.

Victoria. Parliament. *Seventh Report of the Board for the Protection of Aborigines in the Colony of Victoria*. Melbourne: John Ferres, Government Printer, 1871.

Victoria. Parliament. *Sixth Report of the Central Board Appointed to Watch Over the Interests of the Aborigines in the Colony of Victoria*. Melbourne: John Ferres, Government Printer, 1869.

Victoria. Parliament. *The Victorian Hansard Containing the Debates and Proceedings, Legislative Council & Assembly of the Colony of Victoria*. Session 1861–62, vol. viii. Melbourne: Wilson & Mackinnon, 1862.

Victoria. Parliament. *Third Report of the Central Board Appointed to Watch Over the Interests of the Aborigines in the Colony of Victoria*. Melbourne: John Ferres, Government Printer, 1864.

Newspapers

The Age (Melbourne)

The Argus (Melbourne)

The Auckland Star (Auckland, NZ)

Geelong Advertiser (Geelong)

Ovens and Murray Advertiser (Beechworth)

Port Phillip Patriot and Melbourne Advertiser (Melbourne)

Publications

Abbott, Graham J. *The Pastoral Age: A Re-Examination*. Melbourne: Macmillan of Australia, Dalgety Australia Limited, 1971.

Acton, Renae, Peta Salter, Max Lenoy and Robert Stevenson. 'Conversations on Cultural Sustainability: Stimuli for Embedding Indigenous Knowledges and Ways of Being into Curriculum'. *Higher Education Research & Development* 36, no. 7 (2017): 1311–25. doi.org/10.1080/07294360.2017.1325852.

Arkley, Lindsey. *The Hated Protector: The Story of Charles Wightman Sievwright, Protector of Aborigines 1839–1942*. Mentone, Vic.: Orbit Press, 2000.

Attwood, Bain. *The Good Country: The Djadja Wurrung, the Settlers and the Protectors*. Clayton, Vic.: Monash University Publishing, 2017.

Balint, Jennifer, Julie Evans, Nesam McMillan, Giordano Nanni and Melodie Reynolds-Diarra. 'The "Minutes of Evidence" Project: Creating Collaborative Fields of Engagement with the Past, Present and Future'. In *Settler Colonial Governance in Nineteenth-Century Victoria*, edited by Leigh Boucher and Lynette Russell, 203–24. Acton, ACT: ANU Press and Aboriginal History Inc., 2015. doi.org/10.22459/SCGNCV.04.2015.09.

Barry, Amanda. '"A Matter of Primary Importance": Comparing the Colonial Education of Indigenous Children'. In *Rethinking Colonial Histories: New and Alternative Approaches,* edited by Penelope Edmonds and Samuel Furphy, 169–82. Melbourne: RMIT Publishing, 2006.

Barry, Amanda. '"Equal to Children of European Origin": Educability and the Civilising Mission in Early Colonial Australia'. *History Australia* 5, no. 2 (2008): 41.1–41.16. doi.org/10.2104/ha080041.

Barwick, Diane. 'And the Lubras Are Ladies Now'. In *Women's Role in Aboriginal Society*, edited by Fay Gale, 51–63. Canberra: Australian Institute of Aboriginal Studies, 1974. doi.org/10.22459/AH.08.2011.08.

Barwick, Diane. 'Changes in the Aboriginal Population of Victoria, 1863–1966'. In *Aboriginal Man and Environment in Australia*, edited by D.J. Mulvaney and J. Golson, 288–315. Canberra: Australian University Press, 1971.

Barwick, Diane. 'Mapping the Past: An Atlas of Victorian Clans 1835–1904'. *Aboriginal History* 8, no. 12 (1984): 100–31.

Barwick, Diane. *Rebellion at Coranderrk*. Aboriginal History Monograph 5. Canberra: The Australian National University, 1998.

Baylie, W.H. 'On the Aborigines of the Goulburn District'. *Port Phillip Magazine* 1 (1843): 86–88, 137–39, 188–92.

Billis, Ralph Vincent and Alfred Stephen Kenyon. *Pastoral Pioneers of Port Phillip*. Melbourne: Macmillan, 1932.

Blandowski, William. 'Personal Observations Made in an Excursion Towards the Central Parts of Victoria, Including Mount Macedon, Mcivor and the Black Ranges'. In *Papers Reprinted from the Transactions of the Philosophical Society,* edited by the Philosophical Society of Victoria, 1–25. Melbourne: Goodhugh and Trembath, 1855.

Blanks, Harvey. *The Story of Yea: A 150 Year History of the Shire.* Melbourne: Hawthorn Press, 1973.

Bleakley, Alan. 'Animals and Information'. In *The Animalizing Imagination: Totemism, Textuality and Ecocriticism*, 128–55. London: Palgrave Macmillan UK, 2000. doi.org/10.1057/9780230287259.

Bonyhady, Tim. *The Colonial Earth.* Carlton, Vic.: Miegunyah Press, 2000.

Boyce, James. *1835: The Founding of Melbourne and the Conquest of Australia.* Collingwood: Black Inc., 2011.

Bride, Thomas Francis. *Letters from Victorian Pioneers: Being a Series of Papers on the Early Occupation of the Colony, the Aborigines, Etc. Addressed by Victorian Pioneers to His Excellency Charles Joseph La Trobe, Esq., Lieutenant-Governor of the Colony of Victoria.* Melbourne: Trustees of the Public Library, 1898.

Broome, Richard. *Aboriginal Victorians: A History since 1800.* Crows Nest, NSW: Allen & Unwin, 2005.

Broome, Richard. 'Aboriginal Workers on South-Eastern Frontiers'. *Australian Historical Studies* 26, no. 103 (1994): 202–20. doi.org/10.1080/10314619408595960.

Broome, Richard. 'Theatres of Power: Tent Boxing Circa 1910–1970'. *Aboriginal History* 20 (1996): 1–23. doi.org/10.22459/AH.20.2011.01.

Broome, Richard. '"There Were Vegetables Every Year Mr Green Was Here": Right Behaviour and the Struggle for Autonomy at Coranderrk Reserve'. *History Australia* 3, no. 2 (2006): 43.1–43.16. doi.org/10.2104/ha060043.

Butlin, Sydney James. *Foundations of the Australian Monetary System, 1788–1851.* Sydney: Sydney University Press, 1968.

Cahir, Fred, Sarah McMaster, Ian Clark, Rani Kerin and Wendy Wright. 'Winda Lingo Parugoneit or Why Set the Bush [on] Fire? Fire and Victorian Aboriginal People on the Colonial Frontier'. *Australian Historical Studies* 47, no. 2 (2016): 225–40. doi.org/10.1080/1031461X.2016.1156137.

Campbell, Judy. *Invisible Invaders: Smallpox and Other Diseases in Aboriginal Australia 1780–1880.* Carlton South, Vic.: Melbourne University Press, 2002.

Casey, Maryrose. 'Colonists, Settlers and Aboriginal Australian War Cries: Cultural Performance and Economic Exchange'. *Performance Research* 18, no. 2 (2013): 56–66. doi.org/10.1080/13528165.2013.807169.

Casey, Maryrose. 'Performances of Belonging'. *Australasian Drama Studies*, no. 73 (2018): 186–206.

Cato, Nancy. *Mr Maloga: Daniel Matthews and His Mission, Murray River, 1864–1902*. St Lucia, Qld: University of Queensland Press, 1976.

Christie, Michael F. *Aborigines in Colonial Victoria 1835–1886*. Sydney: Sydney University Press, 1979.

Clark, Ian D. *Aboriginal Languages and Clans: An Historical Atlas of Western and Central Victoria, 1800–1900*. Clayton, Vic. Monash Publications in Geography, 1990.

Clark, Ian D. *Goulburn River Aboriginal Protectorate: 'Prettily Situated at Mungalloook', a History of the Goulburn River Aboriginal Protectorate at Murchison, 1840–1853*. Ballarat, Vic.: Ballarat Heritage Services, 2013.

Conor, Liz. '"A Species of Rough Gallantry": Bride Capture and Settler-Colonial Print on Australian Aboriginal Gender Relations'. *Settler Colonial Studies* 3, no. 1 (2013): 6–26. doi.org/10.1080/18380743.2013.761933.

Conor, Liz. *Skin Deep: Settler Impressions of Aboriginal Women*. Crawley, WA: UWA Publishing, 2016.

Darragh, Thomas A. 'William Blandowski: A Frustrated Life'. *Proceedings of the Royal Society of Victoria* 121, no. 1 (2009): 11–60. doi.org/10.1071/RS09011.

de Serville, Paul. *Port Phillip Gentlemen: And Good Society in Melbourne before the Gold Rushes*. Melbourne: Oxford University Press, 1980.

de Serville, Paul. *Pounds and Pedigrees*. South Melbourne: Oxford University Press, 1991.

Elbourne, Elizabeth. 'The Sin of the Settler: The 1835–36 Select Committee on Aborigines and Debates over Virtue and Conquest in the Early Nineteenth-Century British White Settler Empire'. *Journal of Colonialism and Colonial History* 4, no. 3 (2003). doi.org/10.1353/cch.2004.0003.

Fetherstonhaugh, Cuthbert. *After Many Days: Being the Reminiscences of Cuthbert Fetherstonhaugh*. Melbourne: E.W. Cole, 1917.

Fox, Paul and Jennifer Phipps. *Sweet Damper and Gossip: Colonial Sightings from the Goulburn and North-East*. Benalla, Vic.: Benalla Art Gallery, 1994.

Furphy, Samuel. *Edward M. Curr and the Tide of History*. Acton, ACT: ANU E Press, 2013. doi.org/10.22459/ECTH.03.2013.

Grieves, Vicki. 'Aboriginal Spirituality: A Baseline for Indigenous Knowledges Development in Australia'. *The Canadian Journal of Native Studies* 28, no. 2 (2008): 363–98.

Griffiths, Tom. 'How Many Trees Make a Forest? Cultural Debates About Vegetation Change in Australia'. *Australian Journal of Botany* 50, no. 4 (2002): 375–89. doi.org/10.1071/BT01046.

Harris, John. *One Blood: 200 Years of Aboriginal Encounter with Christianity: A Story of Hope*. Sutherland, NSW: Albatross Books, 1990.

Hawdon, Joseph. *The Journal of a Journey from New South Wales to Adelaide (the Capital of South Australia) Performed in 1838 by Mr Joseph Hawdon*. Melbourne: Georgian House, 1952. First published in 1838.

Head, Lesley and Jennifer Atchison. 'Cultural Ecology: Emerging Human-Plant Geographies'. *Progress in Human Geography* 33, no. 2 (2008): 236–45. doi.org/ 10.1177/0309132508094075.

Hegarty, Ruth. *Is That You, Ruthie?* St Lucia, Qld: University of Queensland Press, 1999.

Hiatt, Lester Richard. *Arguments about Aborigines: Australia and the Evolution of Social Anthropology.* Cambridge: Cambridge University Press, 1996.

Holland, Wendy. 'Reimagining Aboriginality in the Circus Space'. *Journal of Popular Culture* 33, no. 1 (1999): 91–104. doi.org/10.1111/j.0022-3840.1999. 3301_91.x.

Hunter, Kathryn M. 'Rough Riding: Aboriginal Participation in Rodeos and Travelling Shows to the 1950s'. *Aboriginal History* 32 (2008): 82–96. doi.org/ 10.22459/AH.32.2011.05.

Hutchinson, Mark. 'The Worcester Circle: An Anglo-Catholic Attempt at Renewal in the 1920s'. *ReVeal: Research@Alphacrucis*, 2010.

Kenny, Robert. 'Broken Treaty: Taungurung Responses to the Settler Revolution in Victoria'. In *Facing Empire: Indigenous Experiences in a Revolutionary Age*, edited by Kate Fullagar and Michael A. McDonnell, 214–35. Baltimore: John Hopkins University Press, 2018.

Kenny, Robert. 'Tricks or Treats? A Case for Kulin Knowing in Batman's Treaty'. *History Australia* 5, no. 5 (2008): 38.1–38.14. doi.org/10.2104/ha080038.

Kerins, Sean. 'Caring for Country to Working on Country.' In *People on Country: Vital Landscapes Indigenous Futures*, edited by Jon Altman and Sean Kerins, 26–44. Leichhardt, NSW: The Federation Press, 2012.

Kerr, John Hunter. *Glimpses of Life in Victoria*. Carlton South, Vic.: Melbourne University Press, 1876.

Kiddle, Margaret. *Men of Yesterday: A Social History of the Western District of Victoria 1834–1890*. Carlton, Vic.: Melbourne University Press, 1961.

Kneebone, Eddie. 'Interpreting Traditional Culture as Land Management'. Paper presented at the Aboriginal involvement in parks and protected areas, Albury, NSW, 1996.

Konishi, Shino. *The Aboriginal Male in the Enlightenment World*. London: Taylor and Francis, 2012.

Lennon, Jane. 'Wrecks and Ruins in the Bush: DCE's Legacy of Industrial History.' *Historic Environment* 8, no. 3/4 (1991): 49–63.

Lester, Alan and Fae Dussart. 'Trajectories of Protection: Protectorates of Aborigines in Early 19th Century Australia and Aotearoa New Zealand'. *New Zealand Geographer* 64, no. 3 (2008): 205–20. doi.org/10.1111/j.1745-7939.2008.00146.x.

Lloyd, Brian E. *Alexandra and District*. Brighton East, Vic.: Historic Publications and Murrindindi Historic Register, 2006.

Long, C.R. 'A History of Alexandra: Part 1. The Beginnings'. *The Victorian Historical Magazine* XVII, no. 2 (1938): 52–63.

Longworth, Alison. 'Upon Past Ebenezers We Built Our Jehovah-Jireh: The Vision of the Australian Aborigines' Mission and Its Heritage in the China Inland Mission'. *Journal of Religious History* 31, no. 2 (2007): 169–84. doi.org/10.1111/j.1467-9809.2007.00552.x.

Mackaness, George, ed. *The Correspondence of John Cotton: Victorian Pioneer, 1842–1849*. Dubbo, NSW: Review Publications, 1978.

McKemey, Michelle B., Maureen Patterson, Banbai Rangers, Emilie J. Ens, Nick C. H. Reid, John T. Hunter, Oliver Costello, Malcolm Ridges and Cara Miller. 'Cross-Cultural Monitoring of a Cultural Keystone Species Informs Revival of Indigenous Burning of Country in South-Eastern Australia'. *Human Ecology* 47, no. 6 (2019): 893–904. doi.org/10.1007/s10745-019-00120-9.

Merlan, Francesca. 'The Mother-in-Law Taboo: Avoidance and Obligation in Aboriginal Australian Society'. In *Scholar and Sceptic: Australian Aboriginal Studies in Honour of L. R. Hiatt*, edited by Francesca Merlan, John Morton and Alan Rumsey, 95–122. Canberra: Aboriginal Studies Press, 1997.

Miller, Jane. 'A Guide to Government Acts, Reports and Regulations Relating to Indigenous Victorians'. *The La Trobe Journal* 85 (2010): 172–82.

Mylrea, P.J. 'Catarrh in Sheep'. *Australian Veterinary Journal* 69, no. 12 (1992): 298–300. doi.org/10.1111/j.1751-0813.1992.tb09909.x.

Nakata, Martin. 'Pathways for Indigenous Education in the Australian Curriculum Framework'. *The Australian Journal of Indigenous Education* 40 (2012): 1–8. doi.org/10.1375/ajie.40.1.

Nanni, Giodano and Andrea James. *Coranderrk: We Will Show the Country*. Canberra: Aboriginal Studies Press, 2013.

Noble, Gerald W. *The Red Gate: A History of Alexandra*. Alexandra: The Council of the Shire of Alexandra, 1969.

Nugent, Maria. 'The Politics of Memory and the Memory of Politics: Australian Aboriginal Interpretations of Queen Victoria, 1881–2011'. In *Mistress of Everything: Queen Victoria in Indigenous Worlds*, edited by Sarah Carter and Maria Nugent, 100–21. Manchester, UK: Manchester University Press, 2016. doi.org/10.7228/manchester/9781784991401.003.0004.

Oliver, Stefanie J. 'The Role of Traditional Medicine Practice in Primary Health Care within Aboriginal Australia: A Review of the Literature'. *Journal of Ethnobiology and Ethnomedicine* 9, no. 1 (2013): 46. doi.org/10.1186/1746-4269-9-46.

Parris, Harry S. 'Early Mitchellstown and Nagambie'. *The Victorian Historical Magazine* xxiii, no. 3: 126–60.

Pascoe, Bruce. *Dark Emu Black Seeds: Agriculture or Accident*. Broome: Magabala Books, 2014.

Pickard, John. 'The Transition from Shepherding to Fencing in Colonial Australia'. *Rural History* 18, no. 2 (2007): 143–62. doi.org/10.1017/S0956793307002129.

Powell, J.M. *The Public Lands of Australia Felix: Settlement and Land Appraisal in Victoria 1834–91 with Special Reference to the Western Plains*. Melbourne: Oxford University Press, 1970.

Ralph-Flint, J. 'Cultural Borrowing and Sharing: Aboriginal Bush Medicine in Practice'. *The Australian Journal of Holistic Nursing* 8, no. 1 (2001): 43–6.

Reed, Liz. 'White Girl "Gone Off with the Blacks"'. *Hecate* 28, no. 1 (2002): 9–22.

Rose, Deborah. 'Love in the Time of Extinctions'. *The Australian Journal of Anthropology* 19, no. 1 (2008): 81–84. doi.org/10.1111/j.1835-9310.2008. tb00112.x.

Rose, Deborah. 'Women and Land Claims'. In *Feminist Ecologies: Changing Environments in the Anthropocene*, edited by Lara Stevens, Peta Tait and Denise Varney, 83–95. Cham: Springer International Publishing, 2018.

Russell, Lynette. '"Dirty Domestics and Worse Cooks": Aboriginal Women's Agency and Domestic Frontiers, Southern Australia, 1800–1850'. *Frontiers: A Journal of Women Studies* 28, no. 1/2 (2007): 18–46. doi.org/10.1353/ fro.2007.0035.

Serle, Geoffrey. *The Golden Age: A History of the Colony of Victoria 1851–1861*. Melbourne: Melbourne University Press, 1963.

Simon, William, Des Montgomerie and Jo Tuscano. *Back on the Block: Bill Simon's Story*. Canberra: Aboriginal Studies Press, 2009.

Smith, Len, Janet McCalman, Ian Anderson, Sandra Smith, Joanne Evans, Gavan McCarthy and Jane Beer. 'Fractional Identities: The Political Arithmetic of Aboriginal Victorians'. *The Journal of Interdisciplinary History* 38, no. 4 (2008): 533–51. doi.org/10.1162/jinh.2008.38.4.533.

Smyth, Robert Brough. *The Aborigines of Victoria: With Notes Relating to the Habits of the Natives of Other Parts of Australia and Tasmania: Compiled from Various Sources for the Government of Victoria*. Melbourne: Government Printer, 1878.

St Leon, Mark Valentine. 'Celebrated at First, Then Implied and Finally Denied: The Erosion of Aboriginal Identity in Circus, 1851–1960'. *Aboriginal History* 32 (2008): 63–81. doi.org/10.22459/AH.32.2011.04.

Strong, Rowan. 'The Colonial Religion of the Anglican Clergy: Western Australia 1830 to c. 1870'. *The Journal of Religious History* 38, no. 1 (2014): 91–114. doi.org/10.1111/1467-9809.12137.

Susemihl, Geneviève. '"We Are Key Players …": Creating Indigenous Engagement and Community Control at Blackfoot Heritage Sites in Time'. In *On Active Grounds: Agency and Time in the Environmental Humanities*, edited by Robert Boschman and Mario Trono. Waterloo, Canada: Wilfrid Laurier University Press, 2019.

Sutherland, Alexander. *Victoria and Its Metropolis: Past and Present*. Edited by R.L.J. Ellery. Melbourne: Today's Heritage, 1888.

Symonds, Sally. *Healesville: History in the Hills*. Lilydale, Vic.: Pioneer Design Studio, 1982.

Thomas, William. *The Journal of William Thomas: Assistant Protector of the Aborigines of Port Phillip & Guardian of the Aborigines of Victoria 1839 to 1867*. Edited and compiled by Marguerita Stephens. Melbourne: Victorian Aboriginal Corporation for Languages, 2014.

Tuck, Eve, Marcia McKenzie and Kate McCoy. 'Land Education: Indigenous, Post-Colonial, and Decolonizing Perspectives on Place and Environmental Education Research'. *Environmental Education Research* 20, no. 1 (2014): 1–23. doi.org/10.1080/13504622.2013.877708.

Twomey, Christina. 'Vagrancy, Indolence and Ignorance: Race, Class and the Idea of Civilization in the Era of Aboriginal "Protection", Port Phillip 1835–49'. In *Writing Colonial Histories: Comparative Perspectives,* edited by Tracey Banivanua Mar and Julie Evans, 93–113. Parkville: University of Melbourne, 2002.

van Toorn, Penny. *Writing Never Arrives Naked: Early Aboriginal Cultures of Writing in Australia*. Canberra, ACT: Aboriginal Studies Press, 2006.

Wards, Ian. *The Shadow of the Land: A Study of British Policy and Racial Conflict in New Zealand, 1832–1852*. Wellington, NZ: Historical Publications Branch, Department of Internal Affairs, 1968.

Watson, Irene. 'Aboriginal Women's Laws and Lives: How Might We Keep Growing the Law?'. In *Indigenous Australians and the Law*, edited by Elliott Johnston, Daryle Rigney and Martin G. Hinton, 15–29. London: Routledge-Cavendish, 2008.

Yarwood, A.T. *Samuel Marsden: The Great Survivor*. Carlton, Vic.: Melbourne University Press, 1996.

Yen, Alan, Conrad Bilney, Michael Shackleton and Susan Lawler. 'Current Issues Involved with the Identification and Nutritional Value of Wood Grubs Consumed by Australian Aborigines'. *Insect Science* 25, no.2 (2018): 199–210. doi.org/10.1111/1744-7917.12430.

Yen, D.E. 'The Domestication of Environment'. In *Foraging and Farming: The Evolution of Plant Exploitation*, edited by David R. Harris and Gordon C. Hillman. North Sydney: Allen and Unwin, 2014.

Yunkaporta, Tyson Kaawoppa. 'Aboriginal Pedagogies at the Cultural Interface'. James Cook University, 2009. Viewed 22 April 2020, researchonline.jcu.edu.au/10974/.

www.ingramcontent.com/pod-product-compliance
Lightning Source LLC
Chambersburg PA
CBHW040820280326
41926CB00093B/4649